# THE
# END OF BRITISH
# PARTY POLITICS?

# THE
# END OF BRITISH
# PARTY POLITICS?

## ROGER AWAN-SCULLY

Biteback Publishing

First published in Great Britain in 2018 by
Biteback Publishing Ltd
Westminster Tower
3 Albert Embankment
London SE1 7SP
Copyright © Roger Awan-Scully 2018

ISBN 978-1-78590-315-1

10 9 8 7 6 5 4 3 2 1

A CIP catalogue record for this book is available from the
British Library.

Set in Adobe Caslon Pro

Printed and bound in Great Britain by
CPI Group (UK) Ltd, Croydon CR0 4YY

# CONTENTS

# ACKNOWLEDGEMENTS

Every UK general election prompts huge amounts of commentary. The electoral analysis industry has never been more vibrant: in addition to the traditional outlets of books, newspapers, magazines and the broadcast media, there is now an ever-expanding universe of online content of various forms (and varying levels of quality).

Understandably, most analysis of elections focuses on the here and now: the election about to happen, currently under way, or recently past. There is always plenty to examine in the present, and plenty of reason to do so. But sometimes it can be valuable to try to step back from the current tumult and see the bigger picture – to examine not only the fascinating detail of the individual trees, but also the contours of the wood that they collectively form.

That is what this book tries to do. While I do spend some time examining the 2017 general election, I locate this vote in a broader historical context. And I examine 2017 not primarily for its impact on who currently resides at 10 Downing Street, but for what the election says about the unity and coherence of the United Kingdom.

Famously, no man (or, indeed, woman) is an island, and certainly no author is. Even a relatively short book like this incurs many debts of gratitude, which I am happy to acknowledge.

May I firstly thank Iain Dale, for believing in this book; and Olivia Beattie and the rest of the team at Biteback for their patience and assistance in getting it to the finishing line.

I would also like to thank the many

professional colleagues, at Cardiff University and elsewhere, and many others with whom I have had the privilege of discussing the ideas in this book.

I am very grateful to my family and friends, for all their love and support.

Most of all, though, I would like to thank the one person who has helped far more, and in more ways, than any other – my wife, the extraordinary Shazia Awan-Scully. *Shukria, meri jaan.*

# CHAPTER ONE

# INTRODUCTION

It was the last party election broadcast before the 2017 general election, and so provided one of the final chances for the party to push its message to the voters. Unsurprisingly, the party chose to make plentiful use of its leader. Confounding many expectations, he had proven to be an effective campaigner over the previous few weeks. Opinion polls had shown his popularity rising consistently since Theresa May had surprised everyone on 18 April by calling the snap election. The leader had defied his critics: he had been front and centre of the campaign, and the party's greatly improved poll ratings suggested that his leadership had worked. Indeed, when the final result a few days later turned out even better than the polls had indicated, the leader emerged a greatly strengthened political figure. The result was widely seen as a personal triumph for him, and those both inside and outside the party who had previously questioned his leadership either fell silent or publicly voiced their praise and loyalty.

I am talking, of course, about the Labour Party leader. But it is not Jeremy Corbyn to whom I refer. I am actually talking about the somewhat less well-known figure (certainly outside Wales, and perhaps even within it) of Carwyn Jones, First Minister of Wales and leader of the Welsh Labour Party. This small example, from the final party election broadcast by Labour in Wales, is one telling illustration of a much broader point – a point which forms the central argument of this book.

Elections are about choices. In a representative democracy, an election is the mechanism

We choose from a menu of options. Political parties provide the options on that menu. Democracy in the UK, and in nearly every other established representative system, remains very much a *party* democracy: organised political movements, which we normally call parties, provide the overwhelming majority of candidates for major elections, and an even greater proportion of those actually elected. As we will discuss later on, political parties in the UK may well have declined in some respects; but their electoral dominance shows no sign of fading.

Of course, we don't always get the menu of options we would like. Lots of people are unhappy with the available choices in most elections. There has been a broad decline in faith in political parties over several decades in the UK, and in many other democracies. Notwithstanding recent surges for the Scottish National Party (SNP) in the wake of the 2014 Scottish independence referendum and the Labour Party around the election of Jeremy

Corbyn as leader, party membership tallies have generally fallen over recent decades. In the electorate as a whole we see a similar picture: far fewer people have a strong and enduring loyalty to, or identity with, a party than used to be the case. Unhappiness with the options available to them is a major reason why many people refuse to participate in electoral politics. But even when it is unsatisfactory to many of us, the menu of options still matters. From one, or some combination, of the available parties a government will be formed after every election.

However, the nature of those electoral menus has changed in a fundamental way. The choices before us were once largely common across Britain. But voters in the UK's four nations are increasingly being presented with fundamentally different, and largely disconnected, sets of political options. We continue to elect one House of Commons – but we do so from four distinct and mostly separate electoral contests. A genuinely *British* democratic politics is being

hollowed out. This book is about how and why
this has occurred, and why it matters.

*   *   *

What unites a country? Perhaps a common
language, maybe a shared religion, or possibly a sense of ethnic similarity. Peoples can
also become more united through facing a
common enemy. But in an important sense,
in a democracy peoples can also be united by
their *differences*. Democracy does not seek to
abolish differences within a society; it merely
provides for their peaceful airing, and their
settling via elections and the other processes
of representative politics. We may not always
get the governments, or the policies, that we
want. But we all get the chance to take part in
the process. And that may allow us to accept
it when we don't get what we want. To work,
democracy ultimately depends on *losers' consent*:
the willingness of the defeated to accept both

the outcome and the legitimacy of the process by which it was reached.

But this 'uniting through our differences' is only likely to occur within a country if the pattern of political differences is broadly similar across the nation. Do we have a common political debate, and a common set of political options? If so, then we may come to feel part of a single political community. If not, an election can become a rather disconnected set of coinciding events in different parts of the country. In the worst-case scenario, political debates may have so little in common that the interests and concerns of different places can appear completely different or even antagonistic, and elections can become a sort of regional or ethnic head count.

This doesn't mean that political health requires that there be no local differences. Rural areas are almost inevitably going to have some different concerns from heavily urbanised ones; rich areas will worry about different things from poorer places. Communities whose economies are heavily dependent on specific industries will have particular concerns that may be little understood elsewhere. Nor does political health require that election results should follow identical patterns everywhere. Indeed, it is pretty much inevitable that different types of populations in different places will mean that the map of electoral results shows at least some variation. During much of the postwar era, as we will discuss in the next chapter, social class was strongly related to how people voted, with the trade-unionised working class being strongly inclined to support the Labour Party. The north of England tended to elect a greater proportion of Labour MPs than the south of England: not because the behaviour of voters was fundamentally much different in the two regions, but simply because a higher percentage of the population in the north were working-class people who were members of industrial trade unions.

The political health of a democratic country probably does require, however, that there be some general unity of political debate, the political options available to people and the electoral choices that they make, across that country. And in the UK this is under increasing threat. The UK has become an electorally disunited kingdom. Electoral choices across Britain have become increasingly differentiated along national lines over much of the last half-century: witness the long decline of Scottish Conservatism, and the rise of the SNP and (to a lesser extent) Plaid Cymru. Such differentiation was shown vividly in 2017: for the second general election in a row, four different parties came first in the UK's four nations.

Beneath this result, and rather less widely noticed, were other developments that pushed party politics in the four UK nations further apart from each other. Northern Ireland has long had a party and electoral politics largely separate from that in the rest of the UK:

electorally Ulster has always been a place apart.
Yet the 2017 election saw the two moderate
forces with the closest ties to the major UK parties, the Ulster Unionist Party (UUP) and the
Social Democratic and Labour Party (SDLP),
lose their last remaining representation in the
House of Commons.

In Scotland the SNP again won the election,
though much less decisively than they had done
in 2015. But the unionist parties achieved their
partial comeback through fighting – albeit with
some success – on the SNP's turf. The defining
electoral issue in the general election in Scotland was independence, and a possible second
independence referendum. All parties, including those most vociferously supporting the
union, fought an election with little connection
to the one occurring in the rest of that union.

Wales offers a more subtle story than the other
non-English nations, reflecting its weaker indig-
enous news media than Scotland or Northern
Ireland, and the closer nature of its social and

economic links with its much larger neighbour. But Labour's successful 2017 campaign in Wales focused almost exclusively on the *Welsh* Labour brand; Jeremy Corbyn was largely excluded from the Labour campaign in favour of Carwyn Jones. After their disappointing result, prominent Tories called urgently for greater autonomy and an identifiable Welsh leader of their party, very much along the lines of Welsh Labour.

Meanwhile, although England and Britain are often conflated by the UK's majority nation, the 2015 and 2017 campaigns both reflected the rise in recent years of a more distinct English identity. After the introduction of English Votes for English Laws in the House of Commons in 2015, all parties felt the need to respond to Englishness as a political phenomenon in their 2017 manifestos.

In short, the 2017 election saw politics across the UK's four nations move further apart – something that was not a one-off, but the further extension of longer-term trends.

Much of our discussion in the next few chapters will involve documenting and explaining these changes in party politics. But we will also be considering their consequences: for voters, for parties and for the UK as a whole.

Voters across the UK's four nations are increasingly faced with general election campaigns that are largely disconnected from each other. At the same time, voters acquire much of their information about the election from news media based in London that display little understanding of these national distinctions, and tend to take events in England as the default setting for UK-wide reporting. This is deeply problematic for many voters' potential understanding of the choices in front of them.

Political parties are also posed problems by the hollowing out of British democracy. Parties are increasingly structured in more complex ways, with different 'leaders' of the UK-wide parties in the different national territories. They also issue increasingly separate manifestos in

Scotland and Wales, and the lines of accountability for delivering on those promises are far
from clear.

The UK continues to elect representatives to
a single parliament. But the shared debates, and
sets of choices, that tie a political community
together are increasingly rare. Indeed, in some
respects the House of Commons increasingly
resembles the European Parliament – whose
members are all democratically chosen, but
from a disconnected series of separate national
electoral contests. This, it will be argued in the
concluding chapter, is deeply problematic for
the long-term unity and integrity of the UK.
In the absence of a genuinely British party politics, the British state may have a limited life
expectancy as a continuing and united entity.

# CHAPTER TWO

# THE ERA OF BRITISH PARTY POLITICS

When talking about a situation where something has changed or even declined over time there can be a great temptation to fall into 'golden age-ism'. That is, to contrast the flawed present with a past where everything was wonderful and just as it should be. That is not my intention here. I come neither to praise nor to bury the past conduct of elections and party politics in the UK. What I do contend, however, is that things are *different*. How British political parties are organised and run, and in particular how they fight elections,

have changed in some fundamentally important ways.

Of course, the manner in which parties fight
elections has changed in lots of ways: witness
this gem about the 1950 campaign:

> Prime Minister, Clement Attlee, undertook a
> 1,000-mile tour around Britain. He travelled
> in his pre-war family saloon car, and was ac-
> companied by his wife (who did the driving)
> and a single detective. If they were ahead of
> schedule they stopped by the roadside and Mrs
> Attlee would catch up on her knitting while
> the Prime Minister did a crossword puzzle
> and smoked his pipe. (Denver et al. 2012: 152).

We certainly don't do it like that any more!
Compared with the immediate post-war elections, campaigning today is very different in all
sorts of respects. Parties make much less use
of the mass meeting or rally than they once
did; moreover, when their leaders do address

audiences in public many if not all of those present are likely to be hand-picked groups of party loyalists, whose main role is not to be convinced by the power of the leader's oratory, but rather to provide an appropriately positive (and, increasingly, an appropriately diverse) backdrop – all for the benefit of the very much larger group of people who may see brief clips of the speech on news outlets or pictures in the newspapers or online. The campaigning efforts of parties are increasingly targeted, focusing on key seats, and differentiated so that individual voters are more likely to receive messages appealing specifically to them. Technological change has opened up numerous other possibilities for the ways in which parties can conduct election campaigns. Just twenty years ago party websites were relatively new and often rather crude affairs, while parties had no need for a social media presence, never mind a sophisticated social media strategy. A great deal has moved on in campaigning in the last

## The Making of British Party Politics

Organised political parties, bearing at least some resemblance to those that exist in the present day, can be traced in the UK back to the mid-nineteenth century. Parties have often been understood as having three main dimensions to their existence: the party in Parliament, the party in the country and the party in the electorate. During the latter half of the nineteenth century, parties in Parliament began to become more organised and disciplined. In the country, local associations, branches and memberships began to take shape in a somewhat more systematic way. And in the (expanding) electorate, parties became a more recognised and influential label influencing voting behaviour, and the objects of varying attitudes from many voters.

As party politics in the UK developed, it was dominated initially by two parties: the Conservatives and the Liberals. In the first election at which large numbers of candidates fought under the Liberal banner, in 1859, the two parties dominated totally, returning every single one of the 648 MPs elected. Their dominance extended across all four nations of the union. The pattern of results was not wholly uniform: on a very restricted franchise, the Liberals won most of the seats in England and Scotland, while the Conservatives narrowly defeated their rivals in both Wales and Ireland. But the competition everywhere involved the same two political forces.

As the right to vote reached a greater proportion of the adult male population during the latter part of the nineteenth century, some differentiation began to emerge in the electoral choices of the various nations of the UK. The clearest example of this was in Ireland. There, up until the 1868 election the main UK-wide parties remained dominant. But in 1874, home rule candidates won the vast majority of Irish seats – only failing to carry the day in much of modern-day Northern Ireland and in the greater Dublin area. The principal losers from this rise of a distinctive Irish partisan force were initially the Liberals: having dominated Ireland in 1868, they now lost all but ten of the sixty-six seats they had previously held. From that point onwards until the creation of the Irish Free State in 1922, the parliamentary representation elected from Ireland (other than from the north) overwhelmingly comprised advocates of Irish autonomy or independence who were not members of the main British parties. Even in their landslide general election victory of 1906, the Liberals made hardly any impact in what had once been a staunch stronghold. The sway of the British parties in most of Ireland was now dead – never to return.

A more subtle picture was seen in the other non-English nations. The Liberals increasingly dominated in Wales from the mid-1860s onwards as the voting population grew. Only in years when the Conservative tide was running particularly strongly across Britain did late-nineteenth-century general elections in Wales look even remotely competitive; in better years for the Liberals, Wales appeared almost like a one-party state. Nonetheless, lopsided though it was, and in growing contrast to Ireland, electoral competition in Wales was conducted between the two main British parties. At the same time, however, Liberalism often had a particularly Welsh tinge. Liberal dominance was grounded in solid electoral support from much of the Welsh-speaking, Nonconformist, *gwerin*.[1] Though never the dominant strand within the party, cultural and political nationalism (even if it might not have been termed such at the time) was an important part of the Welsh Liberal tradition.

The Liberals also dominated in Scotland for much of the latter half of the nineteenth century. But the divisions that the issue of

---

1   The Welsh word *gwerin* does not have a precise English translation, but is generally understood to refer to the 'ordinary folk' of Wales.

Irish home rule provoked in Liberal ranks in the 1880s, and the ability of the Conservatives and their new Liberal Unionist allies to tap into support from Protestant communities in the west of Scotland which maintained strong social and religious ties to unionists in Ulster, saw a notable rise in the number of non-Liberal MPs elected in 1886. In the wake of the failure of Prime Minister Gladstone's final attempt to introduce Irish home rule, the Conservative and Unionist forces came close to parity in the number of Scottish parliamentary seats in 1895, before winning a narrow majority of them in 1900. Nonetheless, these differences between the mainland British nations in voting patterns were ones only of degree. In the great Liberal landslide victory of 1906, the party was almost wholly dominant in Wales and Scotland, but it also won a clear majority of the seats in England – where the Conservatives had so often defeated the Liberals previously.

After the end of the First World War in 1918,

several major changes occurred in the landscape of politics in the UK. First, the nature of
the electorate changed substantially. All adult
male citizens (with adulthood then being ad-
judged to be reached at the age of twenty-one)
were given the vote; women were also rapidly
brought into the voting population. Ordinary
people now all had the chance to choose who
governed over them.

Second, the establishment of the Irish Free
State in 1922 substantially altered the territorial
shape of what became the United Kingdom of
Great Britain and *Northern* Ireland. Irish independence also removed a significant chunk of
MPs from the House of Commons (although
for the last few years most Irish MPs, elected
under the Sinn Féin banner, had refused to take
up their seats). But perhaps most importantly,
the departure of most of Ireland eliminated a
long-standing and deeply divisive issue from
the political agenda. Arguments over Irish
home rule and related matters rather abruptly

disappeared from prominence in British politics, where they had often dominated in the
previous half-century; Ireland was not to return
as a major political issue for almost another
fifty years.

A third major change that occurred in
the years after 1918 was the rapid decline in the
Liberal Party and its replacement as the main
non-Conservative party by Labour. The rise of
Labour happened at a somewhat uneven pace
across Britain. In Wales, whose economy and
society was overwhelmingly dominated by
unionised heavy industries like coal mining,
the party, inextricably intertwined with the
trade union movement, came first in both seats
and votes for the first time at the 1922 general
election – and it has done so at every single
one of the twenty-five subsequent general
elections. England and Scotland were a little
slower to succumb to Labour's charms. Labour
first topped the poll in Scotland in 1923, did
so again the following year and in 1929, but

then failed to win again in Scotland until 1945. In England, it was not until Clement Attlee's post-VE Day landslide that Labour came first in votes (although they narrowly edged out the Conservatives in seats in 1929).

With the rise of Labour also came a change in prevailing attitudes to national distinctiveness within the UK. The Liberals had a long, although far from unqualified, tradition of support for home rule in Ireland, and many Liberals had favoured it being applied across the UK. There were elements of this in the Labour tradition too: Keir Hardie had been a supporter of home rule for Scotland; so also, for some time, were Ramsay MacDonald, the party's first Prime Minister, and later Tom Johnston, the wartime Secretary of State for Scotland. Similarly, there were certainly elements in the Welsh Labour Party that recognised as important the cultural and linguistic distinctiveness of Wales. Such traditions were later to form much of the basis of support for devolution within the

Labour Party. But the dominant strands within the party came to be those which emphasised the politics of class, and the promotion of the common interests of working people across the UK. The politics of nationality was viewed by much of the Labour movement as, at best, a bourgeois distraction from more important matters; after 1945, anything relating to 'nationalism' was often equated with the recently defeated forces of fascism and Nazism.

The wartime years, and those following, also saw a large increase in the power and role of the British state. Government took an increased role in the health, education and social welfare of its citizens, and began to play a much larger role in the economy. Much of this was done in a uniform way across the UK. There was some qualification to this: the devolved government in Northern Ireland ran education and the NHS there; in Scotland, the implementation of policy in both areas was largely the responsibility of the Scottish Office, not of the education or health ministries in London. But these are minor embellishments to the general picture of a greatly expanded British state taking a much larger role in the lives of all its citizens in a broadly common way across the UK.

## The High-Point of British Party Politics

There are various respects in which British party politics can be said to have reached a high-point in the two decades after the Second World War. Party memberships were large: estimates have suggested that as many as 2.8 million people may have been members of Conservative associations in the early 1950s, while just over one million were direct members of the Labour Party (and many millions more were members of trade unions that were affiliated to the Labour Party). Lots of these members were not active political campaigners (just as a large proportion of party members now are not), but political parties also had a much greater social function than they enjoy today: the Young Conservatives were sometimes said to be not so much a political movement as a 'middle-class dating agency', where respectable young people could meet each other in times long before eHarmony or Tinder.

Even among the much larger proportion of the electorate who were not members of any party, there were nonetheless very many who had a settled and deep-rooted sense of identity with one of the two major parties. In a substantial sense they felt that they *were* a Conservative or Labour. When the first detailed surveys of the British electorate were conducted, around the 1964 election, fully 81 per cent of all those surveyed were found to identify with one of the two main parties, and two-fifths of the sample said that this identification was 'very strong'.

The Conservative and Labour parties also dominated electorally. In elections which had high turnouts by more recent standards, the two main parties won a very large majority of the votes and an even greater proportion of the House of Commons seats. There were four general elections held during the 1950s. In none of these elections did the combined total won by all the parties other than the Conserva-tives and Labour, added to the aggregate of all the independent candidates, amount to more than 10.3 per cent of the vote across Britain. Nor were more than twelve non-Conservative or Labour candidates successful at any one of these elections.[2]

In short, the immediate post-war decades were a period in which politics in Britain was dominated by two large parties. These same two parties were represented across Britain, and were the key players in elections everywhere. I'll now explore several aspects of the politics of this period in turn.

---

2 In these aggregates of seat totals Northern Irish Unionists are counted as Conservatives, for reasons discussed later in this chapter.

*Election Results*: Throughout the 1950s and 1960s, the same two parties were electorally dominant in all three mainland British nations. The Liberals still existed, but were now only a relatively minor force: their numbers of MPs remained in single figures until a mini-surge up to twelve in 1966, with most of the few seats that they won being in the 'Celtic fringes' of rural Scotland and Wales and the south-west of England. The dominant parties everywhere were the Conservatives and Labour. Their fortunes were not wholly identical across the three nations of Britain. The Conservatives' historic weakness in Wales persisted; they were clearly stronger in both England and Scotland. Labour consistently experienced its best results in Wales. Beyond the Liberals there were no other remotely significant parties operating across Britain – UKIP and the Greens were not yet even a glint in a psephologist's eye. Meanwhile, within Scotland and Wales respectively, the SNP and Plaid Cymru were very much

Prior to that, electoral changes moved in strikingly similar ways from election to election across Britain.

Figure 2.1: Inter-election Conservative vote share changes, 1950–70

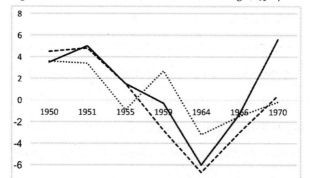

Figure 2.2: Inter-election Labour vote share changes, 1950–70

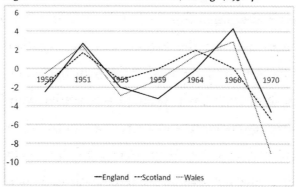

Northern Ireland was, as ever, the exception. It was largely self-governing for half a
century after the secession of the twenty-six
counties that formed the Irish Free State. But
the north remained part of the UK, and elected a small number of MPs to the House of
Commons. In return for enjoying substantial
autonomy, Northern Ireland returned only
twelve representatives at general elections; this
meant that the province was actually slightly
under-represented in relation to population,
whereas Scotland and Wales were always
over-represented. The majority of MPs returned from Northern Ireland at every election
throughout the 1922–72 period were unionists;
they never won fewer than two-thirds of the
seats, and on three occasions actually scooped
all twelve. Electorally, Ulster marched to the
beat of a different drum from the rest of the
UK. (Quite literally so on days of Orange Order
parades.) Yet Northern Ireland was not wholly
disconnected from the politics of mainland

Britain. Unionist MPs sat in the House of Commons as Conservatives, taking the Tory whip. Thus, unionist election victories contributed to broader Conservative successes. The peculiar electoral politics of Northern Ireland thereby retained a connection to the fate of the parties in the rest of the UK.

*Election Campaigning*: During the first post-war decades, as I have suggested already, many aspects of parties' election campaigning were very different from what they would look like today. For the first four general elections after the war, coverage of the campaigns in the broadcast media was very limited. Prior to 1959, impartiality was maintained in broadcast coverage of the election campaign by not having any such coverage! Political parties were given some free air time to put their case – the dreaded party political/election broadcasts, which were first aired on radio and then also on television. Other than that, media coverage of the campaigns was largely confined to the newspapers – which had no requirement to be impartial and in many cases made absolutely no attempt to be so.

The general election of 1959 was, in two senses, the first television election in the UK. By that year the majority of households had a television set, while the broadcast media now provided extensive coverage of the campaign. From then on, the rest of the century saw an ever-increasing focus by political parties on how to present their case to the public via positive media coverage – which meant, most particularly, on television.

Aside from coverage in the mass media, election campaigns came down to parties' own efforts on the ground. All electoral politics was, in a sense, local. But – with the permanent exception of Northern Ireland and the partial exception (discussed below) of the Scottish Unionists – the main political parties ran largely unified campaigns across Britain, under unified leaderships. There were no Welsh and

Scottish 'leaders' of the Labour or Conservative parties, as were seen in 2017. Rather, the leaders and other major figures from the main parties campaigned fully across the different nations of Britain. Historical accounts of the period, and biographies of the major political figures, are replete with discussions of campaign speeches by the party leaders and other prominent figures across the cities and towns of England, Scotland and Wales. And it was quite common for prominent political figures from one of the nations of Britain to find a constituency in another one. Following the much earlier examples of Gladstone (an Englishman with a country estate in Wales who ended up representing the parliamentary constituency of Midlothian in Scotland) and Churchill (also English, but who for some years was an MP for Dundee), both James Callaghan and Michael Foot, English leaders of the Labour Party, served for many years as MPs for constituencies in south Wales.

*Party Organisations*: During this era of the high-point of British party politics, both the Labour and Conservative parties had some degree of 'regional' organisation across Britain. But in each case this machinery was, in the main, very limited. Both the autonomy enjoyed by the regional organisations and their influence over their wider parties were highly restricted.

These limits were particularly obvious in the case of the Labour Party. Labour had eleven 'regional councils' within the overall structure of the party; among these eleven were the Welsh Council of Labour and an equivalent Scottish body. But these were not major decision-making bodies within the party at all. The policy functions of the regional Labour councils were very much limited. Indeed, R. T. McKenzie's classic 1960s study of British political parties reported that 'the regional organs of the Labour Party are precluded from discussing national and international issues unless they have a particular bearing on the region concerned' (McKenzie 1963: 240). The main policy-making machinery of the Labour Party operated on a Britain-wide basis, and the major set-piece occasions at which policy was final-ised were the UK Labour Party conferences (and also the conferences of the Trades Union Congress and the major individual unions).

There was also little or nothing in the way of a professional staffing structure for Labour at the regional level: very few party staff were deployed there, and any that were had their sal-aries paid by, and were directly answerable to, the party headquarters and National Executive Committee, in London. They were employees of the party in London; there were no Welsh and Scottish Labour Party staff to speak of. The structures of Labour's internal leadership and party organisation reflected the then-dominant centralising impulse within the party; the perceived priority of advancing the shared interests of workers and citizens required, it was generally believed, a united party pursuing common policies across the country.

The situation was, with only one substantial exception, little different with the Conservatives. Wales (and Monmouthshire) was one of twelve 'provincial areas' in the Conservative Party. Provincial-level organisation and staffing for the Tories, as with Labour, was very limited. So also was the autonomy and influence enjoyed by the regions. However, the Tories did make at least some greater acknowledgement of local interests, with the Executive Committee of the party's National Union including significant representation from the provincial area party organisations. McKenzie suggested that 'limited though the influence of the Conservative provincial areas may be, it is probable that the work of the Conservative Party at this level has greater meaning for members of the party than is the case with Labour' (1963: 241). But this was 'greater' than almost nothing at all – and even then not by very much. Overall, it is

Another exception, now largely one of the forgotten stories of politics in Britain, concerns the Conservatives in Scotland. Scotland was not one of the Tory Party's twelve provincial areas. There, instead, existed an autonomous and distinct entity: the Scottish Unionist Party. The party had been formed in 1912, from the merger of the previous Scottish Conservatives and the Liberal Unionists, who had been co-operating very closely ever since Gladstone's home rule policy for Ireland had prompted the Liberal Unionists to break away from the Liberal party in the 1880s. Organisationally the Scottish Unionists were a quite distinct entity from the Conservative and Unionist Party in England and Wales; they placed a strong emphasis on the Unionist label, with the 'Conservative' brand widely seen in Scotland as being very much an English phenomenon. Unionists elected in general elections took the Tory whip in the House of Commons – just as did Unionists from Ulster. Yet the Scottish party was much more influential at Westminster: two of its major figures, Andrew Bonar Law and Sir Alec Douglas-Home, became (albeit short-lived) Prime Ministers and party leaders for the Conservatives.[3]

Much of the credo of the Scottish Unionists would appear to contemporary eyes to be very 'British'. Not only did Scottish Unionism share with its counterparts in Northern Ireland a very close connection to Protestantism; both strands also strongly supported not only the union with Ireland but also the British Empire. Yet the Scottish Unionists saw no contradiction between endorsing that and also being in at least some senses intensely Scottish: they rejoiced in and sought to project a distinct Scottish identity, which they often contrasted with the centralising tendencies of the Labour Party. Key Labour policies such as nationalisation were castigated for having the impact

---

3  For the definitive account of the Scottish Unionist Party, see Seawright 1999.

of taking Scottish-owned businesses into the hands of a London civil service; other policies that expanded the role of the state in the provision of social services were criticised for taking control of public services away from Scottish local authorities and putting them into the hands of government in London. Yet as memories of the Irish home rule issue faded, and with the empire also disappearing, the Scottish Unionists' special branding lost much of its relevance. In 1965 the party was merged into the Conservative and Unionist Party, with control now very much being exerted from Conservative Central Office in London.

*Party Policies*: To what extent were different policy agendas followed by the parties across the nations of the UK during the immediate post-war decades? It is very difficult to summarise concisely the entire contents of multiple manifestos across numerous elections, to say nothing of the actions of UK governments between those elections. But a number of things are clear.

Once again, Northern Ireland was exceptional. It enjoyed substantial self-government, and could follow its own path on much of domestic policy. In some respects it clearly was different: for instance, in the multiple ways, often subtle, by which the minority Catholic population experienced political and social discrimination – something that was increasingly regarded as unacceptable on the British mainland. More generally, Northern Ireland was hardly a beacon of innovative or progressive policy making: Ulster Unionism was a conservative creed both constitutionally and socially, and apparently never-ending one-party dominance was hardly a context which demanded radicalism from the province's politicians.

On the British mainland, the main parties allowed their regions (as we have already seen) little if any policy autonomy. The Welsh and Scottish parties did not develop separate policy

programmes or issue wholly distinct manifestos. Rather, amid unified policy programmes,
the local parties might help develop ways of
specifying the local consequences and implications of those policies.

Policies specific to Wales or Scotland were
few and far between. Some Liberal figures
continued to talk periodically about home rule,
or devolution as it later became known, but by
now few cared about any policies that the Liberals articulated. The larger parties took some
time to become nearly so radical. The Conservatives produced a (bilingual) statement of
'Policy for Wales and Monmouthshire' in 1949.
Yet this document was not produced by the
Welsh 'provincial' party, but by Conservative
Central Office.[4] Moreover, the Conservatives
were a long way from advocating any form of
self-government for Wales. When returning to

---

4  One of the Conservative Central Office staff responsible for producing the 1949 statement of policy for Wales is believed to have
   been Enoch Powell, who certainly had at least some knowledge of,
   and ability to speak, the Welsh language.

government in the 1950s, the Tories did create the specific role of a (junior) minister for Wales, and they also designated a Cabinet minister to have special responsibility for looking after Welsh interests. But beyond this, it is difficult to find much evidence of Conservative policies made with Wales specifically in mind.[5]

Centralism and the expansion of the British state was a dominant theme of the immediate post-war Labour government. In the party's thirteen years of opposition from 1951 onwards, they began to rethink. After some years of internal squabbling, Labour eventually moved to support the creation of the post of Secretary of State for Wales: a Cabinet-level position with a supporting ministry. The policy was enacted when Labour returned to government in 1964 – with the first-ever Welsh Secretary being the former deputy leader Jim Griffiths,

---

5  The most detailed study of the Conservative Party in Wales remains that by Tomos Dafydd Davies, 'A Tale of Two Tories?' (PhD thesis, Aberystwyth University, 2011).

by now a political veteran but undoubtedly a major figure within the party. The Welsh Office was initially tiny by Whitehall standards, and had very limited responsibilities. Although it never became anything like one of the great offices of state, as bureaucracies tend to do it slowly accrued greater staff resources and some wider responsibilities. Yet this was only 'administrative devolution'; any serious Wales-wide elected body was not yet a seriously considered proposition.

Scotland had enjoyed such administrative devolution since 1885; moreover, during the inter-war years control over several major areas of policy in Scotland (including health, education and agriculture) was moved from semi-autonomous 'boards' into the Scottish Office. In the hands of an ambitious and able figure, and given sufficient scope by their Prime Minister, the role of Secretary of State for Scotland was thus potentially one of a major policy-making figure in Scottish life. Probably the greatest holder of the role, Tom Johnston, in post from 1941 to 1945, transformed much of the economy of Scotland by using a new Scottish Council of Industry to help attract many hundreds of industrial businesses; set up a swathe of committees to address major long-standing social problems; and even established a prototype national health service several years before Nye Bevan's legislation of the later 1940s. But the role of Scottish Secretary remained in the gift of the UK Prime Minister, and the holder of the role was very much part of a unified system of British government.

## Conclusion

This chapter has documented the high-point of British party politics. The immediate postwar decades were an era when politics was dominated throughout Britain by the same two parties. Those parties not only had large

# CHAPTER THREE

# THE DECLINE OF BRITISH PARTY POLITICS

T he previous chapter documented what I called the high-point of British party politics. If the immediate post-war decades were that high-point, when, how and why has there been a decline? In this chapter I will start to answer those questions, by documenting how a unified British party politics has eroded over recent decades. The growth in electoral distinctiveness of the non-English nations in recent decades will be illustrated with statistical evidence and historical examples. The chapter will also consider how devolution has led to increasing organisational and policy differentiation within political parties in the UK.

## The Electorally Disuniting Kingdom

It started, in a sense, in Carmarthen. The west Wales town is a fairly unremarkable place. But in July 1966 it was the scene of an historic parliamentary by-election. Only a few weeks after the March 1966 general election, the sitting Labour MP for Carmarthen, Megan Lloyd George (the daughter of David Lloyd George, and herself a former Liberal deputy leader before she defected to Labour in the mid-1950s), died of breast cancer. Lady Megan had held the seat comfortably in a general election triumph that had seen Labour score its highest-ever vote share in Wales; her nearest, though not very near, challenger in Carmarthen at that general election had been her former party. It was therefore a major shock when the by-election to replace her saw the seat won neither by Labour nor the Liberals but by Plaid Cymru under their veteran leader, Gwynfor Evans. This was the first peacetime parliamentary breakthrough for either Plaid or the SNP.[6] It was followed the next year by a similar success for the SNP, when Winnie Ewing won in Hamilton (a seat the SNP had not even bothered to contest the year before), and there were several other by-election near misses for both Plaid and the SNP in the following few years.

The years since the mid-1960s have not been ones of unalloyed success for the SNP and Plaid Cymru. That has been particularly the

6  The SNP did win one parliamentary seat in a by-election, in April 1945 in Motherwell, with many voters turning to them as they lost patience with the wartime electoral truce whereby the mainstream parties did not contest each other's seats in by-elections. In the general election that followed shortly afterwards, the SNP lost the seat again to the Labour Party and it did not win parliamentary representation again for over two decades.

case in Wales, where Plaid have never finished better than third in vote share at a general election. But the Carmarthen by-election was the start of a process that changed two things. First, Scotland and Wales became more distinct electoral arenas – with significant parties that did not stand outside those nations, and which sought to define the boundaries of the political community as Scotland and as Wales, rather than as the UK. Second, these initial successes for Plaid and the SNP instigated more serious political debate and consideration about what we now know as devolution. The idea that Scotland and Wales were nations that ought to have that nationhood recognised in significant political institutions of their own was not put into practice straight away – that would take another thirty years. But this idea was transformed from a fringe notion into the political mainstream. The second half of this chapter will explore devolution and its implications for

1945 until 2015.[7] Difficult though it may be to believe today, until 1974 Wales was more electorally distinct from England than was Scotland. This was primarily down to the persisting Conservative electoral under-performance in Wales, and its obverse in continual Labour dominance. The surge in support that the SNP experienced in October 1974 changed all this – at every general election since, Scotland has looked more different from England than Wales has, albeit sometimes only very slightly. Wales's distinctiveness reached a high-point in 1992 – when Labour was led by the Welshman Neil Kinnock (a point discussed further below). Scotland's electoral separateness from England made substantial advances in 2010 and again in 2015 – when very nearly half of those who cast a ballot voted for a party that did not even

---

7   The index of dissimilarity potentially runs from 0 (which would mean political parties gaining exactly the same vote share in Scotland or Wales as in England) to 100 (in which case all the votes would have gone to parties that had won no votes in England). The greater the differences in vote share a party gets between one nation and another at an election, the higher the index score.

exist south of the border. Scotland had become a wholly different electoral space to England.

Figure 3.1: General election 'dissimilarity' of Scotland and Wales from England, 1945–2015

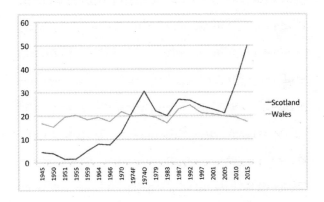

Beneath the overall picture indicated in the chart lie two main types of development. The first is divergence in the fortunes of the main Britain-wide parties across the nations of Britain. The most obvious and substantial element of this is the long decline of the Scottish Conservatives – something which began in the general election of 1959, and continued right up to the general election of 2015, when the party hit a new low in scoring below 15 per cent of the vote for the first time. To reach this level from a vote share of above 50 per cent in 1955 was an extraordinary decline, and one quite unrelated to the fortunes of the Tories in either England – where they continued to prosper – or even Wales, where their long-standing under-performance compared to England has actually tended to diminish slightly since the 1980s. Anti-Conservatism came to appear to be part of the mainstream of Scottish politics – in a way that was initially exploited very effectively by the Scottish Labour Party, but which later came back to bite Scottish Labour when they suffered a political backlash from many of their traditional supporters for having allied with the Conservatives in the September 2014 Scottish independence referendum.

The other major element in the electoral divergence of the nations of Britain in their general election voting behaviour has been the rise of parties that do not compete politically across all three mainland British nations, never mind in Northern Ireland. The key players here are obviously the SNP and Plaid Cymru. Since it made its breakthrough to political relevance with the Hamilton by-election, the SNP have won at least 10 per cent of the vote, and at least one seat, at every general election. This is not to say that it has been progress all the way for the Scottish nationalists. After it surged to 30.4 per cent of the vote in the second 1974 general election, winning eleven seats and coming close in several more, the party experienced many difficult years. At both the next two general elections the party saw its vote share slump, down to only 11.8 per cent in 1983, and they returned only two MPs on both occasions. It was only its remarkable post-independence referendum surge in support that saw the SNP finally, in 2015, come first in votes in Scotland and once more see their number of MPs rise into double figures. What was astonishing about 2015 was the sheer scale of the SNP's advance: they went support at any of them. They have, nonetheless, remained a resilient presence in electoral politics in Wales, and a serious competitor in a number of seats in the rural west and north of Wales. Moreover, Plaid's very existence adds a different dimension to party and electoral politics in Wales. And their occasional surges in support have been a persistent reminder to the Labour Party of the need to guard their cultural and political flank against an alternative party on the centre-left.

Having said all of this, general elections remained wholly dominated by Britain-wide political parties throughout the 1980s and 1990s. After the SNP's false dawn of October 1974, the combined total of nationalist MPs never exceeded ten at any general election until May 2015. Even as late as 2010, with the SNP operating as the single party of devolved government in Scotland (albeit a minority government), it was still viewed as credible and acceptable for the major UK broadcasters, when screening the first-ever televised leaders' debates in the UK, to include in this set of three debates only the leaders of the three main Britain-wide parties: Prime Minister Gordon Brown for Labour, Conservative opposition leader David Cameron, and Nick Clegg for the Liberal Democrats. Other parties were relegated to offering reaction interviews after the debates to the broadcasters and, in the case of the SNP and Plaid, participating in the Scottish and Welsh 'regional' debates with the Scottish and Welsh leaders, or main spokespersons, of the Britain-wide parties. The latter debates attracted much lower audience figures and media attention, even in Scotland and Wales.

By 2015, things had very obviously changed. The one leaders' debate aired on UK-wide television – on ITV, early in the campaign – featured seven leaders, rather than three. This reflected in part the success of UKIP and the Green Party in increasing their support, which led to their inclusion. But the larger stage also reflected the perceived need to include both the SNP and Plaid Cymru. With the SNP polling around 50 per cent in Scotland, and potentially on course to be the third-largest party in Parliament, it was not credible to exclude them. Even though they were only standing in Scotland, they had the clear potential to win sufficient seats to exert substantial post-election influence across the UK. And if Nicola Sturgeon had to be included as SNP leader, so also, it seemed, did Plaid Cymru's leader, Leanne Wood. In the event, both Sturgeon and Wood acquitted themselves capably, as they also did in the somewhat strange 'opposition leaders' debate' broadcast by the BBC (a debate which Prime Minister Cameron voluntarily avoided, and which also excluded Deputy Prime Minister Clegg).

When all the votes had been cast and counted, the 2015 general election result was historic in at least one sense: four different parties had come first (in both votes and seats) in the four nations of the UK. The Conservatives had won in England, as well as across the UK as a whole. But the SNP had come an emphatic first in Scotland, Labour had won yet again in Wales, and the DUP once more led the way in Northern Ireland. This cross-national electoral disparity had never happened before. Never had the United Kingdom appeared electorally more disunited.

For much of the post-war era, there was also little obvious relationship between the nationality of the party leaders and the electoral success of their parties. The Liberals experienced their all-time low in support in Wales (prior, that is, to the new nadir they would reach in 2017), and had sharper drops in general election support there than in either England or Scotland, when they were led by the Welshman Clement Davies for more than a decade from 1945. Labour experienced their all-time high general election vote shares in both Scotland and Wales, but not in England, in 1966 – when

'Falklands factor' in Scotland even as the Tories rampaged to a landslide win elsewhere. For the final seven years of her premiership, Mrs Thatcher's main opponent was Labour's Neil Kinnock, who led his party through both the 1987 and 1992 general elections. Compared with his party's low-point of 1983, Kinnock was able to raise Labour's vote share over these two general elections by exactly twelve percentage points (from 37.5 per cent in 1983 to 49.5 in 1992) within his native Wales; compare this with England, where Labour's support rose only by seven percentage points (from 26.9 per cent to 33.9 per cent); and Scotland, where Labour's 35.1 per cent vote share in 1983 had risen by less than four points (to 39.0 per cent) by 1992.

This was not just a phenomenon peculiar to Neil Kinnock, or to the Labour Party. When Charles Kennedy became leader of the Liberal Democrats, they had won exactly 13 per cent of the vote in his native Scotland at the previous general election in 1997. Kennedy was able to help his party raise this share by very nearly ten full points (to 22.6 per cent of the vote) by 2005, the second of the two elections in which he led his party. The Lib Dems' electoral performance during the same period was notably less impressive in Wales (where they managed to increase their vote share over these two elections by 6.1 percentage points) and England (where the increase was 4.9 points from 1997 to 2005). After Kennedy stood down, the Liberal Democrats actually saw their vote share in Scotland decline in 2010 when they were led by the Englishman Nick Clegg, even as the party made advances in both Wales and England. Meanwhile, and now led by the Scotsman Gordon Brown, Labour actually saw their vote share rise by more than three percentage points in 2010 in Brown's native land, even as the Labour vote share fell by more than six points in Wales and more than seven in England. Though it was hardly the only important factor, particularly outside England the nationality of a party leader now mattered significantly for the relative electoral success of the main Britain-wide parties. This was one clear indicator of Britain becoming a less united electoral and political space.[8]

## The Devolved Kingdom

The political breakthroughs of the SNP and Plaid Cymru in the late 1960s brought forth a response from the UK's political establishment. They established that ultimate stalling device, a Royal Commission on the constitution. The Commission had a very wide remit, encompassing the governance of the whole of the

---

8  Possible counter-examples that could be offered against the idea of the nationality of party leaders having become electorally influential are Tony Blair and Michael Howard: Blair was Scottish by birth (and for at least some of the years of his education); Howard was Welsh both by birth and by upbringing until university. Yet there was no disproportionate surge for Labour in the Blair years, nor for the Conservatives in Wales when Howard led his party at the 2005 election. But both men represented parliamentary constituencies in England, and Blair was not generally viewed as Scottish in the manner that Brown and Kennedy were; nor was Howard viewed or identified as Welsh to anything like the same extent as was Kinnock.

UK as well as the crown dependencies of the Channel Islands and the Isle of Man. As one authoritative account has suggested:

> These last [the crown dependencies] were the giveaway. The Royal Commission was a device not to find the truth or to recommend changes, but to give the impression that the Government was looking at the issue and would not be in a position to make a commitment until after the next general election. (McLean and McMillan 2005: 161)

The Commission outlived its original chair and ultimately failed to agree on its final report. But from its convoluted recommendations emerged the policy which became known as devolution: the creation of elected chambers that would exercise significant self-government for Scotland and Wales, while keeping both firmly within the UK. Devolution was, in many senses, nothing new: Northern Ireland had enjoyed very far-reaching self-government for half a century after its establishment as a distinct entity in 1922.

The path to implementing devolution turned out to be long and tortuous. Years of parliamentary trench warfare throughout the 1974–79 parliament, with the Labour government's own policy facing determined and sustained opposition from a political coalition that included many of the party's own backbench MPs, culminated in the by-now tired and deeply unpopular government putting the matter to the people. On 1 March 1979 (Wales's national day, St David's Day), national referendums were held in Scotland and Wales. The verdict from the Scottish people was ambiguous – a narrow yes to devolution, but failing to clear a threshold of 40 per cent of the registered electorate that Labour opponents of devolution had inserted during the parliamentary passage of the legislation. The decision of the Welsh lacked any ambiguity at all: by nearly a four-to-one margin, people in Wales said no to devolution. Even the strongest Welsh-speaking heartlands voted emphatically against self-government.

There was only a muted reaction in Scotland when Margaret Thatcher's new Conservative government moved a few months later to repeal Labour's devolution legislation. In Wales, the idea of self-government seemed dead: the popular historian Gwyn Alf Williams referred to the Welsh having 'voted themselves out of existence'. The issue was only revived in a serious way after Scotland had turned decisively against the Tories in the 1987 general election: the Campaign for a Scottish Assembly developed a Claim of Right for Scotland, which was publicly signed the following year by the vast majority of Scottish MPs, MEPs and many other major figures in Scottish life. The Claim referred to 'the sovereign right of the Scottish people to determine the form of Government best suited to their needs', and its signing was followed by a wide-ranging three-to-one majority, the latter by almost two to one. In Wales, plans for a much weaker national assembly were put to people a week later; here the verdict was also Yes, but by an achingly narrow margin.[9] Majority public support for devolution in Wales only emerged clearly *after* the institution had been created (Wyn Jones and Scully 2012, chapter 3).

Devolution, as it has been applied in the UK, is not a minor or trivial matter. Probably the greatest British-based political scientist of the last half-century described it as a transfer of powers on 'a scale unprecedented in the history of mainland Britain and possibly without precedent in the history of the democratic world' (King 2007: 347). Among its many implications have been several for party and electoral politics. There have now been five sets of elections to the devolved institutions in Scotland and Wales. In Scotland these have produced a range

---

9   The margin of victory for the Yes campaign in Wales was 6,721 votes – representing a mere 0.3 per cent of the electorate.

of outcomes and a variety of governments: two Labour–Lib Dem coalitions, two SNP minority governments and even an SNP single-party majority administration. In Wales, devolved government has always been Labour led: either as a single party or as the largest party in a coalition involving either the Lib Dems or Plaid Cymru.

Devolution has helped to generate a more complicated, multi-arena electoral environment for political parties in the UK. It used to be the case that general elections to the House of Commons at Westminster were the 'only electoral game in town' for parties – or at least the only such game that mattered. But things have become more complex. We have had European Parliament elections since 1979; there are now a number of significant mayoral elections; referendums have become a more common part of the political landscape in the UK; and in the non-English nations of the UK there are also elections to powerful devolved parliaments. Devolution, in particular, has posed significant questions for parties about their internal organisation and political branding. Power has been devolved within the UK; should it therefore also be devolved internally within parties?

The Labour Party, the midwives of devolution, have gone through a particularly interesting experience in the devolution years. When the Scottish Parliament and Welsh Assembly were first inaugurated, Labour found themselves in power in three capital cities: London, Edinburgh and Cardiff. Now they hold power only in Cardiff Bay. At first, it appeared that the Scottish party would be far the more autonomous, in keeping with the much more far-reaching devolution granted to the Scottish Parliament. The inaugural First Minister, Donald Dewar, was a strong figure who was respected throughout the Labour Party. But after Dewar's untimely death in October 2000, Scottish Labour have experienced a series of weak and uninspiring leaders – both in government up until 2007 and in the decade of opposition that has followed. Throughout much of this period, Gordon Brown – Chancellor and then Prime Minister in the London government until 2010 – was rumoured to exert strong control over the party in his native land. But even several years after Brown had stepped down, one resigning Scottish Labour leader (Johann Lamont) complained that the party in Scotland was treated by headquarters in London as a 'branch office'. Rather than trumpeting any specifically Scottish policies, and the distinctiveness of their approach, Scottish Labour even before the 2014 independence referendum came to be seen by many as the 'tribunes of Westminster', and thus were in a poor political place to respond to the political attacks by their main opponents in the SNP – who argued that they, and not Labour, would more effectively stand up for Scottish interests.

After a very sticky start, the Labour Party in

Wales have managed the politics of devolution much more effectively than have their counterparts in Scotland. In the first devolved election in Wales Labour failed to gain the majority in the National Assembly that almost everyone had expected, in the face of a major advance by Plaid Cymru. (It is now almost universally forgotten that in the first devolved elections the nationalist share of the vote was higher in Wales than in Scotland). Much of that seemed down to the uninspiring leadership of Alun Michael, imposed as putative Assembly leader on Welsh Labour by the party in London. Michael proved no more inspiring once in office, and Labour's political opponents combined to bring him down within a few months. His replacement, Rhodri Morgan, sought both to strengthen devolution for Wales and to make the Labour brand more distinctly Welsh. Rather than the Blairite 'New Labour' approach, Morgan favoured what he termed a 'Classic Labour' agenda and policies, while rule from London by Edward Heath's Conservative government, produced a fracturing of relations between the Ulster Unionists and the mainland Conservative and Unionist party. Ulster Unionist MPs stopped taking the Conservative whip in the House of Commons. Later events, notably the 1985 Anglo-Irish Agreement negotiated by Margaret Thatcher's government, and bitterly attacked by unionists for giving the Irish Republic a say in the affairs of Northern Ireland, further distanced the relationship. Both the Ulster Unionists and the Democratic Unionist Party, which has increasingly come to dominate that side of the great divide in the province, clearly lean towards the right in socio-political terms. But they can no longer be counted on for parliamentary support by the British Conservative Party. As Theresa May discovered in 2017, their support comes at a price.

Overall, devolution has helped impel political parties in the UK to organise themselves in more differentiated ways. Westminster is no longer the sole focus of their activity; the parties must also fight regular elections to Scottish and Welsh political institutions. And experience thus far has suggested that playing the national card – having distinctive and strong Scottish and Welsh leaderships and policy agendas – is the most effective way for the Britain-wide parties to fight these elections. That is a lesson that the Welsh Labour Party learned the hard way very early in the devolution era; it was one that Scottish Labour have had to learn an even harder way in recent years.

## Conclusion: Carry On Brexiting

In June 2016, the UK held a referendum on its membership of the European Union. This vote had been long awaited by many opponents of EU membership, and in the end they won an historic victory: the UK voted to leave.

But the whole of the UK did not vote that way. There were narrow but clear votes for Brexit in England and – to the undisguised consternation of the native political class, who have long cherished a self-image of the Welsh as being more politically progressive and pro-European than their neighbours to the east of Offa's Dyke – also in Wales. But Brexit was rejected in Northern Ireland, where survey estimates suggested that a fairly narrow but clear Leave vote among the Protestant community was outweighed by overwhelming Remain support from the province's Catholics. And the Remain vote was even clearer in Scotland, where the still-popular SNP government campaigned to reject Brexit, a stance that was also very publicly and strongly supported by the Tories' Ruth Davidson. In Scotland some 62 per cent opposed the Brexit that the UK as a whole had now endorsed, and which the government of the new Prime Minister, Theresa May, now set out to try to deliver.

The patterns of voting in June 2016 were very different from those in the only previous similar referendum, in June 1975. In 1975 all four nations of the UK had voted to stay in. Then, England and Wales had been the most pro-European parts of the UK; while Scotland and Northern Ireland still voted for the UK to stay in, they did so a little less emphatically. Now the four nations were split, two for Remain and two for Leave, with England's overwhelming demographic weight meaning that its relatively narrow Leave vote (along with the even narrower one cast by Wales) more than cancelled out the more decisive Remain verdicts delivered in the union's other two nations.

Much has already been said and written about Brexit, and there will be plenty to follow. This book is not about that issue. For our purposes, Brexit is principally relevant for offering a further demonstration of the UK's status as an increasingly electorally disunited kingdom. On this absolutely crucial referendum, the verdict from which put the UK state on course to try and achieve the most complicated and difficult thing that it had done since fighting the Second World War, the country found itself deeply divided. As the government began to try to make Brexit mean Brexit, it did so with some stark divisions at home: between young and old, between the more and less well educated, between cosmopolitan communities and the 'left behind' areas that voted for change. But there were also divisions along national lines – divisions which threatened to give the SNP a convincing pretext for calling a second independence referendum. The people of Scotland had voted within two years to stay within two unions – they were now being told, in effect, that they had to choose between them.

In the months that followed, Theresa May said repeatedly that the UK was 'coming together' behind her government's Brexit policy. There were precious few signs of this from

# CHAPTER FOUR

# GENERAL ELECTION 2017

This was the election that should never have happened. The 2011 Fixed-Term Parliaments Act (FTPA), passed by the Conservative–Liberal Democrat coalition, had legislated for parliaments to last for five years after a general election, and the one elected in 2010 had indeed done so. By spring 2017 it was, of course, not even two years since the previous general election in May 2015. Holding an election in June 2017 required the FTPA to be short-circuited.[10]

Why did this happen? There was no great parliamentary pressure on Theresa May's government. Yes, the Conservatives' paper majority in Parliament was a narrow one – only twelve over all other parties combined. Yet in reality the government's position was much more secure than this suggested. Four of the opposition seats were held by Sinn Féin, who do not participate in Westminster politics. Another eight were held by the Democratic Unionists, also from Northern Ireland, who would often side with the Conservatives in parliamentary votes. Most importantly of all, the main opposition party, Labour, had been a shambles in Parliament for most of the time since the election of Jeremy Corbyn as their leader

---

10 The FTPA still allowed for an early election to be called if a two-thirds majority in Parliament approved it. After Theresa May decided to seek such an early election, Jeremy Corbyn and the Labour Party agreed to support this request. The motion approving the election was therefore passed the following day by 522 votes to 13.

in September 2015. There had been multiple shadow Cabinet reshuffles, and at least one attempted coup against Corbyn by many of his own parliamentary colleagues. A disorganised and divided Labour Party were in no position to provide strong opposition to the Conservatives in Parliament.

Nonetheless, there seemed a compelling political logic to May calling the election. The Conservatives had been well ahead in the polls throughout the nine months since she had entered 10 Downing Street. And there appeared very little prospect that the shambolic Labour Party would prosper, under the active scrutiny of a hostile press, in the intensity of a general election campaign. By calling an early election, May was gambling that she could win big – delivering a substantial parliamentary majority that might provide her with a buffer in the event that the Brexit process turned difficult, the economy suffered a major downturn, or the government was beset by other misfortunes.

But, in truth, election 2017 did not look like much of a gamble – it seemed one of the safest of safe bets.

We now know that it didn't turn out like that, of course. But this is not one of the many attempts to explain 'what went wrong for the Tories in 2017', nor how things turned out much better than expected for Labour. Instead, my focus here is on analysing how the parties sought to fight the election, and the results that it produced.

## The Campaign

With the election coming so unexpectedly, even to most of those in the party that called the early poll, many preparations had to be hurried. Manifestos had to be written speedily and lots of candidates selected at short notice. Still, much of the election proceeded in a very similar way to others in recent times.

parties have long fought elections there, campaigning on issues which often have little resonance – if they are comprehended at all – by parties and voters in the rest of the UK. Thus, the Democratic Unionists gave prime position in their manifesto to the issue of re-establishing devolved government at Stormont (although most of the party's manifesto was at least basically 'devo literate' in the sense of actually relating to matters normally decided at Westminster). Sinn Féin's 2017 Westminster manifesto led on Brexit, but much of the rest of the document highlighted issues, such as education and the health service, that are – at least in 'normal' times – devolved to the province. Theresa May did make a brief campaign visit to Northern Ireland in mid-May. But this visit appeared primarily about highlighting the issue of Brexit (by focusing on the issue of the Irish border, on which the Prime Minister promised that she would deliver a frontier-free border after the UK's departure from the EU):

in short, it was about maintaining a focus on the key issue for the Conservatives in the election campaign on the mainland, not about seeking to influence the result in Ulster itself.

*Wales*: The two largest parties ran very different types of campaigns in Wales. The Conservatives followed a traditional path. In an election for the UK Parliament, they focused attention on their UK leader; the campaign was very much directed from party HQ in London. There was little obvious Welsh leadership to the Welsh Conservative campaign. Indeed, if anyone was leading the campaign in Wales, it was unclear who. There were two televised 'leaders' debates': one on ITV Wales and the other on BBC1 Wales. In the first of these the Conservative case was put by Andrew R. T. Davies, the party's Welsh Assembly leader. Davies's performance was less than stellar: his repetitive overuse of key Tory election slogans, such as 'strong and stable leadership', saw him being openly barracked by audience members from halfway. There was then a bizarre public spat between Davies and the UK government's Welsh Secretary, Alun Cairns, as to who should represent the Conservatives in the second debate: this resulted in neither doing so, and another Conservative AM, Darren Millar, was called upon at rather short notice to participate in the BBC debate (something which Millar did quite capably). Meanwhile, the Conservative Welsh manifesto, *Forward Together*, put a fairly light Welsh gloss on the Conservatives' Britain-wide document, also entitled *Forward Together*. The two documents even looked strikingly similar. For the Conservatives in Wales, at least, election 2017 was mainly fought as a British election.

The approach of Labour in Wales could scarcely have been more different. In 2015, the party's approach had been similar to that of the Conservatives in 2017. The Welsh manifesto sketched out the Welsh implications of the

Britain-wide document, while the party's case in the two televised Welsh debates was put by the shadow Welsh Secretary – and later party leadership contender – Owen Smith. In 2017, there was no doubt who was leading the party's campaign in Wales. It was not Jeremy Corbyn; nor was it shadow Welsh Secretary Christina Rees. First Minister Carwyn Jones – a rarely seen figure in the general election just two years previously – was front and centre of the entire campaign. Jones spoke for Labour, very effectively, in both televised debates. The Welsh manifesto was this time rather more than just a Welshed-up version of the Britain-wide document, *For the Many, Not the Few*. *Standing Up for Wales* looked very different from what the party in London had produced. Closer scrutiny of the details of the document showed rather more commonality of key themes. But, at least for the casual observer, everything was seemingly designed to emphasise that this was a Welsh Labour document wholly distinct from the manifesto that the party in London was campaigning on.

This distinctiveness was also evident in much of the campaigning material used by Labour in Wales. Four Labour party election broadcasts were aired during the official campaign period. Viewers in Wales never, in any of these slots, saw anything produced by the party in London. Not once did they even see the face, or hear the voice, of Jeremy Corbyn. Carwyn Jones figured prominently throughout; the final broadcast, shortly before polling day, closed with a lengthy appeal from him that heavily pushed the party's Welsh credentials. The dominant label used throughout was not Labour, but *Welsh Labour*, and the broadcasts appealed to voters to stop 'the Tories walking all over Wales'. There were also clear attempts to generate resentment against 'Westminster' in ways that came close to the sort of material produced in recent times by the SNP. Leaflets and other material sent to voters had a similar emphasis. Even I, living in anglicised

*Scotland*: The Conservative campaign in Scotland contrasted sharply with that in Wales. In the previous year's Scottish Parliament election, the Conservatives had come second in a Scottish election for the first time in many years, and ahead of Labour for the first time in many more. They had done so through a campaign which focused far more on the personality of their media-savvy Scottish leader, Ruth Davidson, than on a Conservative brand which remained toxic to much of the Scottish electorate. The Tory 2016 campaign had also been based on an uncompromising defence of the union between Scotland and the rest of the UK: that meant steadfast opposition to any second independence referendum. After the relative success of this approach in 2016, a very similar one was followed by the Conservatives in 2017. While the Scottish Conservative manifesto looked very similar to the UK and Welsh versions, it featured a strong early foreword from Davidson which focused heavily on her chosen ground: that 'only by voting for the Scottish Conservatives can people take on the SNP – and say no to their referendum'.[11] This emphasis was constantly reiterated in the Scottish Tory campaign, particularly by Davidson herself.

The SNP had much less wind in their sails than two years previously. In 2016 the party had narrowly lost their majority in the Scottish Parliament, despite their constituency vote share actually increasing slightly. Polls suggested that public enthusiasm for independence had ebbed somewhat; any zest for having another referendum on the matter was even lower. It was certainly understandable that much of the Scottish public might lack enthusiasm for re-fighting the independence referendum: after all, the previous three years had produced two general elections, one Scottish Parliament election, an independence referendum, the Brexit

---

[11] Scottish Conservative and Unionist Party (2017), p. 7.

referendum, plus European Parliament and local council elections. If ever there was a scenario calculated to induce voter weariness with politics, this was it. At the same time, the SNP's opponents had heavily attacked their record in government on key policy issues, especially education. It was notable that independence and a possible second referendum featured much less in the SNP manifesto and campaigning than it did in the campaigns of its opponents – and particularly that of the Scottish Tories. The SNP's main emphasis was on austerity and public services; on the constitution they focused on 'more powers' for the Scottish Parliament, not their ultimate constitutional goal of an independent Scotland.

In Scotland, both Labour and the Liberal Democrats were clearly on the same side of the key electoral dividing line as the Conservatives in 2017. Scottish Labour leader Kezia Dugdale's foreword to her party's 2017 manifesto balanced attacks against both the SNP and the Conservative government in London. The party's first election broadcast of the campaign focused heavily on the divisions in Scottish society that it claimed had been opened up by the independence issue, and the need to bring Scotland back together. In general, there was rather less of a 'nationalist' tone about Scottish Labour's campaign in 2017 than there was from their Welsh colleagues. But the assumption that Scotland was a distinct political and electoral space requiring a distinct campaign was shared by all the major parties in 2017.

*England*: For the 2015 general election campaign, the Conservatives had published a separate English manifesto. For 2017 the party did not do so. But they, like all the parties, felt compelled to discuss England and Englishness to a much greater extent than would have been the case until very recently. The Conservative manifesto celebrated the introduction of (one form of) English Votes for English Laws

(EVEL) to the House of Commons; the document also argued rather vaguely that Brexit had the potential to strengthen the union of the UK as a whole (a theme that was not stressed by the Tories in less Europhobic Scotland), and talked further about developing the Conservative agenda of devolution to city-regions within England.

The Labour Party made one clear policy commitment: to appoint a minister for England, albeit below Cabinet rank, within the Communities and Local Government department. The party also talked of restoring regional structures – mainly established under the 1997–2010 Labour government and abolished by the Conservative–Liberal Democrat coalition. Labour, along with the Liberal Democrats, also proposed a UK-wide constitutional convention – something that Welsh First Minister Carwyn Jones had been calling for, with little apparent effect, for several years.

UKIP, aware that – notwithstanding their

Union Flag waving – much of their electoral support in recent years had come from voters who emphasised an English rather than British identity, proposed the establishment of an English parliament. But after the Brexit referendum, and minus Nigel Farage, few were listening to them now. The confusion of the Liberal Democrats' rather shambolic election campaign was perhaps symbolised by their offering support for EVEL, but then suggesting that this should somehow operate on a proportional basis (within a House of Commons that is still elected under the first past the post electoral system).

Overall, the election saw four quite different campaigns across the four nations of the UK. For Northern Ireland this was nothing new. For the nations on the British mainland, things had moved further. Scotland remained a different political arena from further south – something that even the unionist parties now clearly accepted as an electoral reality. In Wales, the

Conservatives tried to fight a traditional British campaign. But for the eventually victorious party the campaign was all about *Welsh* Labour. The campaigns directed by the parties in London were largely relevant only to England.

## The Results

*Northern Ireland*: In Northern Ireland, the 2017 general election moved electoral politics further in the broad direction that it has been travelling for most of the years since the 1998 Good Friday Agreement. Within the two main communities in the province, the more moderate parties – the Ulster Unionist Party and the SDLP – have tended to lose ground to harder-line voices, as represented principally by the Democratic Unionist Party and Sinn Féin. In 2017 this trend continued, as the UUP and SDLP's electoral support eroded further, such that both of them barely topped 10 per cent of the popular vote and also lost their last representation in the House of Commons. The three remaining SDLP seats, and the two that had still been held by the UUP, were swept away by their harder-line competitors. Northern Ireland's elected parliamentary representation at Westminster is now wholly composed of DUP and Sinn Féin MPs, except for one (unionist) independent, Sylvia Hermon (herself a former UUP member) (see Table 4.1).

Table 4.1: 2017 Results: Northern Ireland

| Party | % vote (change on 2015) | Seats (change) |
|---|---|---|
| Democratic Unionists | 36.0 (+10.3) | 10 (+2) |
| Sinn Féin | 29.4 (+4.9) | 7 (+3) |
| SDLP | 11.7 (-2.2) | 0 (-3) |
| Ulster Unionists | 10.3 (-5.8) | 0 (-2) |
| Alliance | 7.9 (-0.6) | 0 (±0) |
| Others | 4.6 (-3.7) | 1 (±0) |

Northern Ireland politics has not been entirely about a move to the extremes in the last two decades. The cross-community Alliance Party of Northern Ireland has generally increased its support in recent years: at the Northern

Ireland Assembly election at the beginning of March 2017 the Alliance improved their vote share by more than two percentage points. But in the June general election even the Alliance fell back slightly, as the forces of moderation were overwhelmed by those representing less compromising points of view.

For the purposes of this book, however, the main consequence of the general election in Northern Ireland was that the two parties with the closest past or present links to the main British parties were wiped out. Although Northern Ireland's electoral landscape has always been a place apart from that on the mainland, both the UUP and the SDLP have had long-standing links to the Conservatives and Labour respectively. Even now, the UUP's Member of the European Parliament, James Nicholson, sits in the same parliamentary group as the Conservative MEPs. While the post-election deal between the Conservatives and the DUP may presage some longer-term form of association, this appears unlikely: it is far more likely to prove a short-term marriage of convenience for both sides.

*Wales*: In Wales, the 2017 general election result was, in a sense, very predictable. Labour won in Wales – for the twenty-sixth time in a row. As they have done in every general election since 1922, Labour got the most votes and the most seats (see Table 4.2). The last person to defeat Labour in a general election in Wales was David Lloyd George – and he had just won a world war.

Table 4.2: 2017 Results: Wales

| Party | % vote (change on 2015) | Seats (change) |
|---|---|---|
| Labour | 48.9 (+12.1) | 28 (+3) |
| Conservatives | 33.6 (+6.3) | 8 (-3) |
| Plaid Cymru | 10.4 (-1.7) | 4 (+1) |
| Liberal Democrats | 4.5 (-2.0) | 0 (-1) |
| Others | 2.5 (-13.9) | 0 (±0) |

However, the route to this latest Labour triumph was less predictable than many had been.

The first two Welsh polls of the campaign had given the Conservatives significant leads. Only during the campaign did Labour begin to re-assert their traditional dominance. Whether such a development was a consequence of Labour's heavily Welsh-focused campaign, or whether it simply followed the broadly similar trends observable in the polls across Britain, remains a moot point.

That Labour should prove resilient in Wales should come as little surprise: a party does not remain dominant somewhere for nearly a century without having some staying power. More surprising was the sheer extent of the Labour comeback in Wales, after the party had seemed to be facing disaster early in the campaign. Labour ended up scoring their highest vote share in Wales since the first Tony Blair landslide victory of 1997. And far from losing seats – even, as had seemed possible at the start of the campaign, seeing totemic seats in the south Wales valleys under threat – Labour

As two-party dominance reasserted itself in Wales, as in England, the other parties found themselves squeezed. Plaid Cymru's campaign gained little public traction, and their vote share was their lowest in twenty years. The party did actually gain a seat, but they only captured Ceredigion very narrowly, and they held on to their Arfon seat by a similarly tiny margin. Barely more than one hundred voters changing their minds across these two seats would have seen Plaid slip down to two MPs, which would have been their lowest total in a general election since 1983. But Plaid's insipid performance was a positive triumph by comparison to those of the Liberal Democrats and UKIP. As in 2015, the Welsh Lib Dems managed the impressive feat of doing even worse than their colleagues in England and Scotland: at 4.5 per cent, their pathetic vote share was their lowest ever in Wales, and they were wiped out in terms of MPs for the first time since the Liberal Party had emerged in the mid-nineteenth century.

Yet even the Liberal Democrats' performance looked good when compared to that of UKIP. In 2015, UKIP had stood candidates in every seat in Wales, and every one had gained the 5 per cent vote share needed to retain their deposit. Two years later, every single UKIP candidate lost their deposit, as the party shed more than five out of six votes that it had won in Wales in 2015.

Overall, Wales saw fairly similar vote share changes for the two main parties as did England. But this result was arrived at via a campaign where the long-dominant, and ultimately victorious, party had focused on a heavily Wales-centric campaign.

*Scotland*: In Scotland the results were rather paradoxical. The SNP emerged from the election as the clear winner: they were well ahead of the other parties in seats and votes, and continued to have a clear majority of Scotland's representation in the House of Commons. Yet the election was treated as a defeat for them, and for their broader agenda of independence. The SNP's opponents, none of whom won even half as many seats as the SNP, were treated as victors (see Table 4.3).

Table 4.3: 2017 Results: Scotland

| Party | % vote (change on 2015) | Seats (change) |
|---|---|---|
| SNP | 36.9 (-13.1) | 35 (-21) |
| Conservatives | 28.6 (+13.7) | 13 (+12) |
| Labour | 27.1 (+2.8) | 7 (+6) |
| Liberal Democrats | 6.8 (-0.8) | 4 (+3) |
| Others | 0.7 (-2.3) | 0 (±0) |

The 2017 general election actually saw the SNP's second-best ever performance in terms of Scottish vote share, and their second-best ever outcome in terms of seats won. The problem for the SNP was that 2017 came after their extraordinary triumph two years previously, when in the wake of the independence referendum they had won half the entire vote and all but three of the parliamentary seats. (Moreover, even in the three seats that they lost, the

SNP only narrowly missed out.) It was always going to be difficult for the SNP to match that performance in any subsequent election – the only way was down. In fact, the party came very close to slipping even further: they won by only two votes in North East Fife, and by a mere twenty-one in Perth & North Perthshire. In two Glasgow seats, the SNP also held on by fewer than 100 votes. Moreover, not only did the SNP lose twenty-one seats; they also lost some major political figures. Former party leader Alex Salmond was unseated in Gordon; their impressive Commons' leader and deputy party leader, Angus Robertson, was deposed in Moray.

The largest advance was made by the Scottish Conservatives. In 2017 they won their greatest number of Scottish MPs since 1983 and their highest vote share in Scotland since Margaret Thatcher's first triumph in 1979. After a similar performance in the previous year's Scottish Parliament election, 2017 confirmed the Tories as being the second party in Scottish politics, something that would have been difficult to imagine until recently. But the election also represented some progress for Scottish Labour: after disastrous performances in 2015 and 2016, 2017 saw their vote share rise slightly, and they made six seat gains. Even the Liberal Democrats, who had been relegated to fifth place in the Scottish Parliament election the year before, made three seat gains from the SNP – although, as elsewhere in Britain, their vote share actually declined from their dreadful 2015 performance. As had also been seen in Scottish local elections over the previous two years, there appeared to be a significant amount of unionist tactical voting, with some voters willing to turn locally to whichever party was best placed to defeat the SNP.

The 2017 election thus saw a significant unionist electoral comeback in Scotland. The SNP remained the largest party, but they were no longer all-conquering as they had been just two years before. The advances in vote share for the main unionist parties, particularly the Conservatives, made Scotland look a little less electorally distinctive than it had done in 2015. But this occurred, as discussed previously, through those unionist parties fighting a very different election to the one south of the border. Much of the campaign, and in particular the successful emphasis of the Scottish Tories, had been on independence – and their steadfast opposition to an independence referendum. They had fought the SNP on the SNP's turf – and, to at least some extent, had been successful in doing so.

*England*: As is nearly always the case, the outcome of the general election was primarily decided in England. In our highly unbalanced union, the majority nation comprises around 84 per cent of the population and returns exactly 82 per cent of the MPs to the House of Commons. Even though the Conservatives have electorally done much worse in Scotland for more than half a century, and in Wales for more than a century and a half, Labour have never won a secure parliamentary majority at a general election without also winning a clear majority of the seats in England.

The loss of the Conservative parliamentary majority in the 2017 general election was therefore mainly an English failure. The Tories actually made net gains elsewhere – their loss of three Welsh seats being more than compensated for by their twelve Scottish gains. It was the net loss of twenty-two seats in England which meant that Theresa May's next administration would be a minority government (see Table 4.4).

Table 4.4: 2017 Results: England

| Party | % vote (change on 2015) | Seats (change) |
|-------|------------------------|----------------|
| Conservatives | 45.6 (+4.6) | 297 (-22) |
| Labour | 41.9 (+10.3) | 227 (+21) |
| Liberal Democrats | 7.8 (-0.4) | 8 (+2) |
| UKIP | 2.1 (-12.1) | 0 (-1) |
| Others | 2.7 (-1.7) | 1 (±0) |

This net loss rather disguised a greater than usual 'churn' in seats between the main parties. The Conservatives actually captured six seats from Labour, as well as one each from UKIP (Clacton, where Douglas Carswell stood down) and the Liberal Democrats. Yet the Tories also lost twenty-eight seats to Labour, and five to the Lib Dems: bar the three Welsh seats lost to Labour, all of these changes occurred in England. (The only seat changes in Scotland involved SNP losses). This patchwork quilt electoral geography reflected an electoral landscape that had changed substantially – much of it seemingly in response to the previous year's Brexit referendum. Detailed individual-level analysis of voting behaviour suggested that how people voted in 2017 showed a number of differences with such behaviour in the past:

- Social class differences had never been less important to how people voted. Conservative and Labour support levels differed very little across the major social class groups.

• Age had never been more important to voting decisions, with younger people leaning strongly to Labour and older voters being much more favourable to the Conservatives: such had long been the typical pattern, but the extent of it in 2017 was well beyond anything seen before. Data from a very large sample by YouGov put the Conservative vote share at only 19 per cent among eighteen- and nineteen-year-old voters, but at 69 per cent among those aged seventy and above (Curtis 2017).

• Education had also never been more important, with less well-educated voters – who had tended to back Brexit – leaning towards the Conservatives, and university-educated voters favouring Labour.

The political differences opened up by the Brexit referendum had, it appeared, shifted some groups of voters from their traditional patterns of party support. The types of people who had voted for Brexit – older, white and less well-educated voters than the average – swung towards the Conservatives; younger and better-educated voters moved substantially towards Labour. This pattern of individual-level behaviour, then, had implications for the types of seats where the parties did relatively well. The Conservatives lost both Kensington & Chelsea and Canterbury to Labour – results that would once have been unthinkable. Yet the Tories gained Mansfield and North East Derbyshire in the post-industrial East Midlands.

There were still distinct geographical patterns to the distribution of seats in England. The Conservatives did much better in rural and semi-rural areas, while Labour was strong in urban constituencies. To some extent these long-standing patterns were actually reinforced by the growing relevance of age and education to voting decisions. England also shared with Wales the marginalisation of the minor parties in the 2017 general election. Although the Liberal Democrats made two net gains, their performance overall was very patchy, their overall vote share fell on their dreadful 2015 performance, and in many seats their vote was utterly derisory. UKIP's performance was almost universally dire. The Greens retained their single parliamentary seat, in Brighton. But while their MP there, Caroline Lucas, proved a far more effective media performer as party leader than had Natalie Bennett in 2015, the Greens were not able to translate this into widespread votes: with Corbyn's appeal meaning that many previously disaffected leftists moved back to Labour, the Greens' vote share fell by more than half on that in the previous general election.

## Conclusions

General election 2017 was extraordinary in many respects. The campaign and the result seemed to overturn, or at least challenge, a whole range of collective wisdoms about how general elections in the UK work – some of them the product of decades of diligent scholarly research. Prior to Theresa May deciding to hold the early election, the following were widely accepted:

- *The UK was witnessing a long-term decline in two-party politics.* Since the high-point of the collective dominance of the Labour and Conservative parties in the 1950s, there had been a steady and substantial cumulative decline in the share of the vote won by these two parties at general elections. This decline reflected a long-term erosion of the importance of social class ties to political parties: the days when the overwhelming majority of working-class people voted Labour and middle-class people voted Conservative are now well in the past. The proportion of people in Britain with a deep-rooted and long-term attachment to one of the main parties – a sense that they 'are' a Conservative, or Labour – is also much lower than it was a few decades ago. By 2010, the decline of the two main parties had reached the point where between them they could not win two-thirds of the votes cast in the general election. Even with the collapse in 2015 of the Liberal Democrats – who had, for much of the previous half-century, been the main beneficiary of votes cast by people who had lost faith in the larger parties – the big two saw only a slight resurgence, as support surged for UKIP and, in Scotland, for the SNP.

- *The election campaign period rarely sees significant changes.* As scholars have documented in extensive – possibly even excessive – detail, the formal campaign period between the dissolving of Parliament and election day very rarely sees substantial changes in party support. One academic has described election outcomes as a 'pre-baked cake' (Wlezien 2016): polls months ahead of an election generally provide a pretty reliable guide to which way things are going to go. The attitudes to politics and the parties that push people to vote one way or another are shaped over several years by major news events, and by perceptions of the performance of governments on the big issues. The efforts of the parties during the formal campaign period largely cancel each other out; often the most useful thing parties can do is simply to concentrate on mobilising the support of those already well disposed towards them. Such was even the case in the 2010 general election. The Liberal Democrats famously saw their support surge after Nick Clegg's strong performance in the first televised leaders' debate. Yet in the end the 'Cleggasm' yielded little if any electoral payoff for the Lib Dems: the short-term surge in support had dribbled away by polling day, and against nearly all expectations Nick Clegg's party actually ended up making a small net loss in seats, rather than gaining ground.

- *Divided parties don't prosper in elections.* It has long appeared to be the case that the public does not react well to political parties that are obviously divided or that clearly have little confidence in their party leader. The largest modern-day general election defeats suffered by either the Labour Party (in 1983) or the Conservatives (in 1997) came after each had experienced years of internal public squabbling and the active undermining of their respective leaders. This did not augur well in 2017 for the Labour Party: its leader, Jeremy Corbyn, had been very publicly spurned by the majority of his MPs.

- *The Labour Party does not prosper electorally when led from the left.* The textbook case for this argument has long been taken to be the 1983 general election. Led by the veteran man of the left, Michael Foot, and standing on a leftist manifesto infamously described by the moderate Gerald Kaufman as the 'longest suicide note in history', Labour were smashed. They did little better four years later, even after Neil Kinnock had smartened up the party's presentation and taken on the hard-leftists of Militant. Yet under the centrist Tony Blair, Labour won its two largest parliamentary majorities ever in 1997 and 2001. Of course there was more to it than that: Tony Blair was lucky to face the Tories at their weakest for nearly a century. But the basic lesson that Labour did better under moderate leadership still appeared valid.

All of these apparent truths about electoral politics in the UK seem now to have been overturned. In the wake of the 2017 election outcome, one of the country's leading political scientists summed up the collective bafflement of the supposed experts: 'It's not easy being a Professor of Politics. Everyone expects me to know what's going on and what's likely to happen. But I'm just as bamboozled as everyone else by the outcome of the UK's recent general election.' (Flinders 2017)

But some things are fairly clear. One is that, particularly in the period since the economic crash of 2008, voters in many established democracies have been increasingly willing to contemplate supporting political options that are outside the mainstream of traditional politics. With established ways of doing politics looking flawed and failing to deliver the goods for many ordinary people, more radical options on the right or left, or independent centrists, have sometimes achieved hitherto unthinkable election results. In Greece and Spain, parties of the hard left in the form of Syriza and Podemos respectively have challenged strongly; in Germany the right-wing Alternative for Germany became the third-largest party in the 2017 election; and in France independent Emmanuel Macron beat the far right's Marine Le Pen in the presidential run-off, with the candidates of the traditional mainstream established parties nowhere.

Mainstream centre-left parties have struggled particularly badly in many countries in the last decade. A more flexible working environment, and public sector austerity in many countries, have undermined the social basis of much mainstream centre-left support among unionised, often public sector, workers. And with little public money available to spend, the policy agenda of the centre-left has faced broader problems of credibility, while such parties have generally also struggled to convincingly respond to public concerns about immigration. One response to the struggles of the traditional centre-left has been the rise of more hard-line voices: offering to address people's problems of falling living standards via radical challenges to capitalism, rather than the moderate reforms offered by traditional social democrats. What has been unusual about Britain, Labour and

Jeremy Corbyn is that the challenge to the moderate centre-left has come from *within* the traditional mainstream party, rather than as an alternative to that party. But in Britain, as elsewhere, many voters have been far more willing to respond positively to such positions than they might have been in the past.

The other thing that is abundantly clear from the 2017 general election is the increasing fragmentation of the UK electoral arena into its constituent nations. Never has the UK experienced a general election where the campaigns across the four nations were so ill-connected; an election which to a large extent operated as four separate and merely coinciding political contests. In 2017 we saw very little of a genuinely British electoral and party politics.

For Northern Ireland this was, of course, business as usual. But the parties with closest links to the mainstream ones in Britain lost their last remaining seats. And while advances were made by the DUP, who affirm a strongly

British identity, that form of Britishness is little recognised within Britain itself today.

In Scotland, the election largely became a contest about a second independence referendum. In a sense, it was therefore about Britain and its preservation as some sort of united political entity. Yet it was thus largely disconnected from the contest happening in the rest of the country. The unionist parties were playing on the SNP's turf of debating Scotland's constitutional status; they did so with some success, yet ironically in doing so they further distanced Scottish political debate from that in the rest of the kingdom that they earnestly wish Scotland to remain a part of.

Even in Wales, so long closely integrated with its much larger neighbour to the east, there were large and important changes from previous elections. The Labour Party had learned from recent experience that, even in difficult times, the Welsh Labour brand still had strong purchase with many voters. Facing what initially looked like a very tough election, and in particular a contest between Theresa May and Jeremy Corbyn that seemed most unlikely to favour Labour, Labour in Wales sought to make the campaign as Welsh as possible. To what extent that campaign ultimately accounted for Labour's successful result remains uncertain. But that result left Carwyn Jones and the more 'autonomist' wing of the party in Wales greatly strengthened, and had some Welsh Conservatives looking to emulate the Labour (and Scottish Conservative) model.

The campaigning of the main 'British' parties was largely focused only on England. Of course, that does mean 'only' 82 per cent of all the seats in the House of Commons. But whether consciously or not, the parties headquartered in London have permitted their effective mission to narrow, and a genuinely British electoral and party politics to become hollowed out. The final chapter of this book will consider the broader implications of this development.

CHAPTER FIVE

# THE END OF BRITISH PARTY POLITICS? THE CONSEQUENCES

S o far this book has been devoted to making the argument that party and electoral politics in the UK are becoming increasingly divided along national lines between the different constituent nations of the kingdom. But if this argument is accepted, then at least three further sets of questions are raised:

- Why has this happened? What have been the major forces leading party politics in this direction?

- Will this trend persist? Or is it simply a set of short-term coincidences that could very easily go into reverse? And can something be done about it?
- Finally – so what? Does the decline of a genuinely British party politics, if that is what we are witnessing, actually matter? What are the important consequences that do, or could, follow from it?

This final chapter of the book will be devoted to answering these questions.

## Why?

Why has party politics in the UK moved in the direction described so far? As with pretty much all political change, there is a mixture of short-term, contingent factors and deeper longer-term forces at work.

The short-term factors, many of which might

be seen almost as accidents of history, are potentially almost infinite in number. But among the more obvious ones that can be mentioned are the following:

- The discovery of large deposits of oil in the North Sea at the end of the 1960s – which transformed the potential economic prospects of an independent Scotland, and gave the first serious and sustained boost to the support of the SNP. But for this freak of geology, perhaps the SNP would never have become a major party in Scottish politics, and the political pressure for Scottish self-rule – whether partial with devolution, or full independence – would never have become so substantial.

- The tragic accident that killed Donald Dewar, the inaugural First Minister of Scotland, in 2000, and triggered the series of weak leaders that bedevilled the Scottish Labour Party over the ensuing decade and a half, greatly to the benefit of their main opponents, the SNP.

- The coincidence within the SNP of a generation of leadership figures of extraordinary political talent: Alex Salmond, John Swinney and Nicola Sturgeon. Although Scottish Labour's problems helped open the door for the SNP, the latter had the right people in place at the right time to take advantage of the political opportunities that were presented to them. This helped push the SNP to a series of electoral victories and produced the 2014 independence referendum – developments which collectively changed the entire landscape of Scottish politics.

- The Welsh Labour Party, in 2017, facing apparent electoral disaster, seizing on a heavily Wales-focused campaign and the relative popularity of Carwyn Jones as a potential defensive shield against a UK-level political landscape that had looked very unpromising for them.

- The Scottish Conservatives (and, to a lesser extent, the other unionist parties in

Scotland), discovering in 2016 and 2017 that the politics of 'Indyref 2' could play at least as well electorally for them as they had done for the SNP.

But beneath these, and other, short-term factors and accidents of history are some longer-term and deeper forces. Of these, the most important at play are changing ideas about nation and union within the UK.

Northern Ireland, as ever, is something of an exceptional case. Its politics have long been substantially different, and separate, from those both in mainland Britain and in the rest of Ireland. But Northern Irish politics have grown further apart. In part this is a consequence of the 'Troubles', which gave politics there an overwhelming focus with no equivalent elsewhere in the UK. But another important factor has been the decline in old-style Protestant unionism on the British mainland. Though the Orange Order still lingers on in a few parts of Scotland, and one or two isolated places in England, their activities – and the broader ideas that underpin them – are viewed with at best baffled incomprehension, and often utter abhorrence, by most people in Britain. That sort of Britishness is something that most of us in the UK want absolutely no part of.

Among the British political elite, a 'primordial unionist' attachment to the link with Ireland has almost entirely disappeared. One major study described John Major as the last figure with such attitudes in British politics (McLean and McMillan, 2005): actually, that is probably unfair to Major, whose approach to Northern Ireland (and arguably the rest of the UK) was more subtle and nuanced than this.[12] But there is certainly little or no primordial attachment

---

12  It seems unlikely that a genuinely 'primordial unionist' could have signed the Downing Street Declaration, in which the UK government stated that it had no 'selfish or strategic interest' in Northern Ireland. This prompted the backbench Tory MP for Wolverhampton South West, Nick Budgen – who certainly was a primordial unionist – to ask John Major at Prime Minister's Questions in December 1993 whether he could 'reassure my constituents that the United Kingdom has an interest in maintaining Wolverhampton in the Union'.

to possessing even a part of Ireland in Westminster today; indeed, the vast bulk of the
political and governmental elite would be quite
happy to be rid of any responsibilities there.
The Ulster Unionist Party came to be alienated
from their old links to the Conservatives, largely through the various moves by Conservative
UK governments (the imposition of direct rule
and the Sunningdale Agreement in the 1970s;
the Anglo-Irish Agreement in the 1980s; and
the 1993 Downing Street Declaration) towards
a position of effective neutrality on the future
status of Northern Ireland. It is unlikely that
the 2017 confidence-and-supply agreement between the Democratic Unionists and Theresa
May's government will be much more than a
short-term marriage of convenience.

Nationalists in Northern Ireland have, of
course, never really wanted to be integrated into
British politics anyway. They aim for a united
Ireland. But the SDLP managed at least some
cooperation with the Labour Party for many

years, both at Westminster and in the European Parliament. Indeed, the party arguably had closer links with the British Labour Party than with its rather less successful Republic of Ireland equivalent. But the SDLP are now a shadow of their former self; all of their former House of Commons seats were captured – although not taken up – by Sinn Féin in 2017.

A rather different kind of nationalism is central to understanding the more recently emerging centrifugal trends in electoral and party politics across the rest of Britain. After two decades of devolution for Scotland and Wales such self-rule has become normal for many people. Indeed, there is a substantial cohort of the population – growing with every day that passes – who cannot remember life before the existence of a Scottish Parliament and a Welsh Assembly. Its normality these days, however, should not disguise from us that the central assumption underpinning devolution – that the national identity and status of Scotland

and Wales ought to be reflected in powerful representative institutions for self-government – was at one point very much a fringe, even at times eccentric, notion.

Of course ideas of 'home rule' for Scotland and Wales have a long history; they formed part of some of the schemes for keeping all of Ireland within the union that were developed in the nineteenth and early twentieth centuries. Home rule all round seemed, to some, a way of squaring the circle. After most of Ireland left the union these ideas dropped down the political agenda, though there were some attempts to revive them – notably the Parliament for Wales campaign and the Scottish Covenant Association in the 1950s. Such ideas were also pushed from within the (until the late 1960s, tiny) ranks of the SNP and Plaid Cymru. But this remained very much a minority position for much of the post-war era.

Such is very much no longer the case. I'm not going to discuss here the road to devolution in

Scotland and Wales. What matters for now is that it happened – and it has consequences. Among those consequences is that Westminster is no longer the sole significant centre of political attention and focus: voters and parties in Scotland and Wales can also focus on Holyrood and Cardiff Bay as key political arenas. They may come to view Scotland and Wales, rather than the UK, as the relevant political space in which they operate. In Scotland, in particular, this has already occurred to a significant extent. As the (pro-union) political journalist Chris Deerin observed in autumn 2017:

> Since devolution, the political conversation north of the border has almost wholly unhitched itself from the one in the south. Of course, this was sort of true during the Thatcher era too, but back then both sides were at least arguing about the same things being done by the same people, if often from different ideological starting points. Today, Brexit

apart, the Scottish media and Holyrood's politicians usually pay little notice to what happens at Westminster, other than to sneer or whinge. The nation has its own priorities, its own tribunes, its own targets and its own routes of achieving (or not achieving) them. (Deerin 2017)

Of course how you respond to the fact of devolution is not necessarily a given. Since the Scottish Parliament and National Assembly for Wales were first elected and inaugurated in 1999, different approaches have been taken, sometimes within the same party. At the onset of devolution Labour was in power in London, Edinburgh and Cardiff. The initial approach taken by Labour's first leader in the Welsh Assembly, Alun Michael, was a 'minimalist' one: he was overwhelmingly loyal to the UK leader, Tony Blair, and to the 'Blairite' policy agenda. By deliberate contrast Michael's successor, Rhodri Morgan, carved out a more distinct

Welsh policy agenda (sometimes termed 'Clear Red Water') and gradually pushed for an extension of devolved powers for Wales. Labour in Scotland travelled rather in the opposite direction. Having started out under the leadership of self-described 'cultural nationalist' Donald Dewar, Labour in Scotland became identified with loyalty to the party in London. It is obvious that it is the Welsh Labour approach, taken even further by Morgan's successor, Carwyn Jones, which has proven to be the more politically successful. And it is precisely the success of that approach which means that it is likely to be emulated and taken further.

## Here to Stay?

Is the hollowing out of British democracy discussed in this book a development that is not merely important but also long-term? We all know that what goes up must come down, and that markets can fall as well as rise. Until 2017, one of the strongest and clearest developments in UK electoral politics for the previous half-century or more had been the decline in two-party dominance. Then, in the June 2017 general election we saw the highest two-party vote share since 1970. If that trend can go into dramatic – though possibly only temporary – reverse, then so too can others.

So might our electorally disunited kingdom become more united once more? Well, it *could* happen. The SNP's partial decline in 2017 might go much further, and voting patterns across at least the three mainland British nations might become more uniform once again. It is certainly possible that Brexit might generate new voter alignments in ways that cut across what have hitherto been more typical divisions. We have already seen how, partly it appears in response to the June 2016 Brexit vote, the 2017 election generated probably the starkest divides ever in voting patterns by age group and by education level; at the same time, the traditional British dividing line of social class has never been less important to explaining how people voted. New divisions might follow from Brexit, or some other major events, and these could potentially manifest themselves across all the British nations in ways that reduce the electoral differences between those nations. We may become more of a common electoral space once again.

And yet this does not seem very likely. We know that the main parties in Northern Ireland are not likely to integrate into the British ones, while those UK parties that have made any recent attempts to field candidates in the province (the Conservatives and UKIP) have failed miserably. We know also that devolution to Scotland and Wales is not at all likely to go away. The broad trend over the last two decades, indeed, has been for it to go substantially further. This cannot continue indefinitely, of course: at some point, an entity becomes so autonomous that it is effectively independent. Moreover, the UK government's legislative plans for Brexit, published in autumn 2017, were fiercely attacked by the devolved governments in Scotland and Wales as a 'power grab' – an attempt to at least partially reverse devolution. But it will be politically very difficult, particularly in Scotland, for any such reversals to be both substantial and permanent.

We know further that there is little sign among the people of the kingdom of any desire for the re-creation of Britishness in any wider sense. Neither the 2011 census, nor the various detailed social surveys that are conducted, point to any popular revival of Britishness. If anything, they suggest the reverse – including in England, where a popular sense of English identity has broadly been on the rise. Notwithstanding their waving of the Union Flag (and also their very brief surge of support in Wales), UKIP's brief period of success involved them tapping effectively into the votes of people who prioritise their English identity over their British one – and who tend to be deeply unhappy about the state of both of England's unions, the UK and the EU.

Even in Wales, the trend of the parties is towards greater distinctiveness. In the wake of the Welsh Tories' 2017 election disappointment, the leader of the party in the National Assembly spoke of the need for greater autonomy for the party in Wales and clearer Welsh leadership. Meanwhile, a former minister in the Welsh government actually put forward the idea of the Welsh Labour Party splitting from the UK party over the issue of Brexit.[13] Given the success in 2017 of the Conservatives under Ruth Davidson in Scotland, and Labour under Carwyn Jones in Wales, those parties and their opponents are not very likely to push in the opposite direction.

---

13  Brexit could prompt Welsh–UK Labour split', BBC News, 30 July 2017, http://www.bbc.co.uk/news/uk-wales-politics-40754812 (accessed 11 January 2018).

Perhaps some towering political figures of great GB-wide appeal will arise, in ways that reunite British voting patterns and perhaps even lead to a reassertion of Britishness. But there is precious little sign of such individuals at present. A far more likely way in which the fragmentation of British electoral and party politics could come to a conclusion would be if it results in Scottish independence.

## The Consequences

So does all of this matter? If we are increasingly an electorally disunited kingdom – then so what? I would argue that this development matters for the voters across the UK who cast the ballots; for the political parties that fight the elections and then seek to deal with the consequences of the results; and, ultimately, potentially for the UK as a whole.

*Voters*: For the voters, the developments that have been discussed in this book raise an obvious question: what exactly are we voting for? Of course *formally* nothing has actually changed. In a general election each of us who casts a ballot does so in our local constituency, participating in the choice of one of the members of the House of Commons. A general election is, in a sense, simply 650 simultaneously held by-elections. But in practice we all know that there is much more to it than that. A generation of diligent academic research has shown that local campaigning in British general elections does make a difference, sometimes even enough to turn defeat into victory (or vice versa) at the constituency level. But the main factors shaping how people vote in general elections have long been understood to be national-level politics and the national campaign.

But what are national politics and the national campaign? What, indeed, is 'the nation'? It is not self-evidently the UK. Actually it has never really been that: Northern Ireland has long been politically a place apart, and for half a century after its foundation in 1922 was largely self-governing. But the modern era of devolution, and the increasing differentiation of party organisation and election campaigning documented in the last two chapters, pose problems for voters.

For English voters, who are after all the substantial majority, these problems may be less acute. They will receive much of their news about politics and an election campaign from London-based media, supplemented perhaps by regional news and local newspapers. Policies outlined in the main UK manifestos will generally apply to them. English voters may well struggle, though, to understand the extent of 'variable geometry' that applies to the role of the UK government: its effective writ sometimes applies to England alone, sometimes to England and Wales, and sometimes to the whole UK. They may fail to appreciate, for instance, that under the single NHS brand in the UK are four different health systems. English voters may also be mystified, or at least annoyed, by the presence in election debates of parties like the SNP and Plaid Cymru that have no electoral presence in England.

For voters in the UK's non-English nations, life is potentially much more confusing. From the London-based media that many of them still consume, they will largely hear about the UK-wide parties and leaders, and often about policies that do not actually apply to them. Some two decades into the modern era of devolution, the London-based media still struggle to deal with or reflect very basic elements of this part of the way the UK is governed. The 'regional' and local media in Scotland, Wales and Northern Ireland will tend to show a quite different election from that seen in England, and may often be more 'devo-literate'. But the parties themselves can often seek to blur lines of accountability. In 2017, the Welsh Labour manifesto contained key pledges on education, health and transport. But all of these related to matters that were already devolved. They were therefore already under the control of the Labour Welsh government, and could not conceivably be decided by the outcome of the UK general election.

Voters across the UK continue to use general elections to elect representatives to a single House of Commons. But they do so in what increasingly are four separate elections: with separate leaders, and separate manifestos producing four disconnected sets of simultaneous choices. The shared debates, and the shared sets of choices, that tie a political community together and help to give it a sense of being a coherent and united nation are increasingly absent. How can there be a sense that 'the people have decided', when elections increasingly produce four sets of decisions by four politically distinct peoples? Much of this is fairly old news to people and politicians in Northern Ireland. But for the rest of the UK this is territory that we are having to become used to inhabiting.

*Parties*: The hollowing out of British democracy also poses problems for political parties. These problems are less acute for those parties that only organise within one of the UK's minority nations. A Scottish-focused election is natural terrain for the SNP; a Welsh-focused one similarly so for Plaid Cymru. It is generally much better for them – both in terms of their longer-term political objectives and in terms of their short-term relevance to voters – that the attention in elections is not all placed on Britain-wide parties and a UK-wide political agenda. The recognition that the SNP and Plaid received in the 2015 televised leaders' debates, which was continued in 2017, was a great advance for these parties from the situation in 2010, when there were three televised set-piece debates between the leaders of the then three main British parties.

Yet a politics focused more on the constituent

nations of the UK may not always be an unalloyed good for the nationalist parties. The SNP was able to play on this focus with enormous success in 2015, in the wake of the 2014 independence referendum: it promised to be 'Stronger for Scotland', and ensure delivery on promises of more autonomous powers. Although having its second-best ever general election result in 2017, the SNP experienced a significant setback, finding that a distinctly Scottish-focused general election could be a double-edged sword. A concentration on independence, and particularly the possibility of a second independence referendum in the wake of the Brexit referendum, actually worked to the benefit of the 'unionist' parties – and in particular the most avowedly unionist of them all. The Scottish Conservatives had their best general election result for thirty-four years. Meanwhile, Plaid Cymru's attempts to position themselves as the most resolute defenders of Wales were completely surpassed by Welsh

Labour: the latter very effectively 'out-natted the nats', and portrayed themselves more convincingly as the most effective political voice for this one of the UK's four nations.

As far as the major Britain-wide parties are concerned – well, it is hardly news to suggest that they will seek to tailor their message most effectively to particular groups of voters. In recent years this has been done increasingly with targeted direct mail, and now it is also done with things like Facebook advertising. Parties 'segment' their message, and seek to appeal in the most effective ways to particular groups of voters. And one of the main ways in which parties can look to segment is by nation within the UK. But having distinct leaders in different nations, and campaigning on separate (and not necessarily consistent) manifestos means something rather more fundamental than simply segmenting a message.

For parties that fundamentally believe in the UK as a union, having distinctive party

organisations and election campaigns challenges the ways in which they might conceive
of that union. This ought to be easiest for the
Liberal Democrats: their predecessor parties
long championed devolution (or home rule as
it was once known), and the Lib Dems themselves were established as a federal party. But in
practice, the party has found federalism rather
difficult to practice *internally* – never mind
coming up with a workable scheme to apply
the principle to the UK as a state (Evans 2014).

Labour have long since had internal tensions
about how to relate to the internal differentiation of the UK. Much of the Labour tradition
is deeply uncomfortable with relating to no-
tions of nation at all. The party founded by Keir
Hardie (himself a strong supporter of Scottish
home rule) has been home both to strong opponents of devolution (see, for instance, Neil
Kinnock's numerous and vociferous inter-
ventions on the issue during the 1970s) and
to deeply impassioned advocates of the idea

(including Kinnock's successor as Labour leader, John Smith). In Scotland, Labour delivered devolution – but then became the 'Tribunes of Westminster': rarely taking a highly distinctive policy line during the years when the party was in government in both London and Edinburgh, and in recent years being reluctant to support substantially more devolution. Labour's own Scottish leader, Johann Lamont, talked prior to the 2015 election of being treated as a 'branch office' by London. Lamont's short-lived successor, Jim Murphy, at least talked a much better game about autonomy for the Scottish Labour Party; yet on the broader issue of political autonomy for Scotland as a whole, the party has continued to appear ambivalent. Its proposals to the post-referendum Smith Commission were strikingly unambitious.[14]

---

14 For a comparison of the different parties' submissions to the Smith Commission, and a summary of the final report, see 'The Smith Commission Report – Overview', SPICe Briefing 15/03, 8 January 2015, available at http://www.parliament.scot/ ResearchBriefingsAndFactsheets/S4/SB_15-03_The_Smith_Commission_Report-Overview.pdf (accessed 11 January 2018).

In Wales, the devolution years have seen, at the very least, substantial differences across the Labour Party in levels of enthusiasm. In the years leading up to the 2015 general election, shadow Welsh Secretary Owen Smith and most Welsh Labour MPs remained distinctly 'devo-sceptic'; First Minister Carwyn Jones, supported by many of his AMs, was thinking much more radically not only about devolution but even about the shape of the UK as a whole – proposing a UK-wide constitutional convention to recast the entire nature of the union. Such differences persist within Welsh Labour, although after the 2017 election the 'Carwyn faction' appeared distinctly in the ascendant.

For the Conservative and Unionist Party, the hollowing out of British democracy would appear to pose an existential threat. Yet, in practice, the Tories have in the past often proven surprisingly adaptable to fundamental changes in the nature of the UK. The party was at the forefront of determined opposition to

Irish home rule for decades – but then adapted to full independence for (most of) Ireland with scarcely a missed heartbeat. The party that most strongly believed in the British Empire (fairly) willingly dismantled most of it after the Second World War. And the Tories' long-standing staunch opposition to Scottish and Welsh devolution melted away rapidly in the wake of the 1997 referendums. It is entirely in keeping with this flexible tradition that the Scottish Tories have been quite prepared to fight the threat to the union in Scotland by embracing the strong Scottish leadership offered by Ruth Davidson. Things have been more ambivalent in Wales – reflecting the distinctly 'anglicised' nature of much of the party's support and membership. But the Conservatives' Welsh Assembly leader from 1999 until 2011, Nick Bourne, showed that the party could develop a more authentically Welsh appeal, and future successors may well choose to follow that path.

The increasing differentiation of party

organisation, leadership and campaigning makes life more complicated for 'British' political parties. Segmenting a message by nation is one thing (although the coordinating of messages across nations may at times prove problematic for parties); delivering on separate and potentially contradictory manifestos is quite another. In a sense, the problems faced by the parties are the problems of the UK: how do you make practical sense of a union that is both highly asymmetrical and deeply unbalanced? But the parties that believe in that union will have to find a way of making it work.

*The United Kingdom*: Perhaps most importantly of all, the increasingly disparate nature of general elections constitutes dangerous territory for the future of the UK. If, instead of having common debates about a unified set of issues, we are having largely separate debates across our four nations, there is a growing risk of mutual incomprehension. The issues that animate and drive political debate in one or more of the UK's minority nations may be little, if at all, understood by English politicians. Yet these issues, including the Northern Ireland peace process and the further development of de-volved governance in both Scotland and Wales, are both complex and important. And while we remain within a single state, the actions of pol-iticians at Westminster will continue to have implications for all parts of the UK – even if some of those implications are the unintended spill-over consequences of decisions made for England only. Meanwhile, the separate na-tional political arenas and agendas still have to intersect at times, even in the era of devolution: as seen in 2017 with the confidence-and-supply agreement between the Conservatives and the DUP.

Ironically, given the UK's vote to leave the European Union, our elected chamber of the Westminster Parliament has in at least some senses increasingly come to resemble the EU's own elected chamber, the European Parliament. The parliament's members are all democratically chosen – but from an almost wholly disconnected set of separate electoral contests across the EU's various member states. There is thus very little sense that European Parliament elections provide the people of Europe with any significant opportunity to choose between different visions of European governance; indeed, it is difficult for most people to perceive any obvious EU-level consequences of these elections at all.[15] It is therefore hardly surprising that turnouts in these elections, which were never very impressive, have tended to decline since the parliament was first elected

---

15 In an effort to generate some clear Europe-wide consequences to European elections, the major European party federations in 2014 each nominated potential candidates for the Presidency of the European Commission; the idea was that the European elections would be viewed as at least in part a choice between these *Spitzenkandidaten*. This attempt to bring a unified focus to European Parliament elections was at best only a qualified success, although the lead candidate of the largest party group in the European Parliament after the election, Jean-Claude Juncker of the centre-right European People's Party, did end up as the next European Commission President.

in 1979. Many Britons, and perhaps particularly many Brexiteers, will shudder at a comparison between the Strasbourg/Brussels multilingual roadshow and the supposed 'Mother of Parliaments'. Yet in relation to the politics of their election, the comparison appears increasingly justified. Although clear UK-level consequences still follow from UK general elections, those elections themselves are increasingly disconnected across the kingdom's four nations.

If UK general elections continue on their current path, this ultimately is potentially problematic for the long-term unity and integrity of the UK. Political unions are fragile things – this, at least, is something that citizens of the first member state to vote to leave the EU should be able to understand very well. The British state is an entirely contingent entity: though it may feel very much 'natural' to all of us who have never known anything else, its existence is not in any sense necessary or inevitable.

Indeed, that state has been through much

more turbulence than many accounts would have us believe. Those who emphasise what Churchill termed 'the long continuity of our institutions', traced back through the mythical 'mists of time', tend to ignore the major convulsions that have transformed the fundamental political geography of these islands roughly once every century since the time of King Henry VIII.[16] The formal incorporation of Wales into the kingdom of England in the early sixteenth century was followed at the beginning of the seventeenth century by the union of English and Scottish crowns, as the ill-fated Stuart line came south from Edinburgh to assume the English throne from the now defunct Tudors; there was then the formal parliamentary union between Scotland and England in 1707; a similar union between Ireland and Britain in

---

16 It should also be noted that the list of major convulsions discussed here relates only to the *geographical* shape of the state and its borders. I thus do not touch upon other major transformative events – such as the civil wars that saw Charles Stuart deposed by Oliver Cromwell, nor the later final overthrow of the Stuart monarchs by William and Mary of Orange.

1800; and the independence of twenty-six of Ireland's thirty-two counties as the Irish Free State in 1922. Less than a century ago, the UK lost a greater proportion of its core territory – through Irish independence – than Germany had lost only a few years previously via the Treaty of Versailles. And less than five years ago, the UK narrowly avoided what was not so much another bullet as a large piece of artillery munition, when perilously close to half of those voting in Scotland opted for independence. The political history of what is now the United Kingdom of Great Britain and Northern Ireland is not remotely the story of continuity and stability that many would like to think it is.

The UK may continue to stay together – fragmentation is by no means inevitable. But the absence of a genuinely British party politics that would generate a sense of a unified political community by linking us into common political debates and decisions certainly does not help. We could end up not merely as an electorally disunited kingdom. The British state may have a limited lifespan as a continuing and united entity. The end of British party politics could well mean the end of Britain itself.

# REFERENCES

Curtis, Chris (2017), 'How Britain voted at the 2017 general election', YouGov, 13 June 2017, https://yougov.co.uk/news/2017/06/13/how-britain-voted-2017-general-election/ (accessed 10 January 2018).

Davies, Tomos Dafydd (2011), 'A Tale of Two Tories?' (PhD thesis, Aberystwyth University).

Deerin, Chris (2017), 'Britain's Brexit toxicity is pushing the Scots away', *New Statesman*, 27 October.

THE END OF BRITISH PARTY POLITICS?

Denver, David, Christopher Carman and Robert Johns (2012), *Elections and Voters in Britain* (Basingstoke: Palgrave Macmillan).

Evans, Adam (2014), 'Federalists in Name Only? Reassessing the Federal Credentials of the Liberal Democrats – An English Case Study', *British Politics* 9, 346–58.

Flinders, Matthew (2017), 'A glorious defeat: anti-politics and the funnelling of frustration', Election Analysis, http://www.electionanalysis.uk/uk-election-analysis-2017/section-2-voters-polls-and-results/a-glorious-defeat-anti-politics-and-the-funnelling-of-frustration/ (accessed 11 January 2018).

King, Anthony (2007), *The British Constitution* (Oxford: Oxford University Press).

McKenzie, R. T. (1963), *British Political Parties: The Distribution of Power within the Conservative and Labour Parties* (2nd edn, London: Heinemann).

McLean, Iain and Alistair McMillan (2005), *State of the Union: Unionism and the Alternatives in the United Kingdom Since 1707* (Oxford: Oxford University Press).

Scottish Conservative and Unionist Party (2017), *Forward Together: Our Plan for a Stronger Scotland, a Stronger Britain and a Prosperous Future.*

Seawright, David (1999), *An Important Matter of Principle: The Decline of the Scottish Conservative and Unionist Party* (Aldershot: Ashgate).

Wlezien, Christopher (2016), 'The (Mostly) Pre-baked Cake: Polls and Votes', in Philip Cowley and Robert Ford (eds), *More Sex Lies and the Ballot Box: Another Fifty Things You Need to Know About Elections* (London: Biteback).

Wyn Jones, Richard and Roger Scully (2012), *Wales Says Yes: Devolution and the 2011 Welsh Referendum* (Cardiff: University of Wales Press).

© GERAINT BRAMWELL

# ABOUT THE AUTHOR

Roger Awan-Scully is an expert on elections and political representation in Britain and Europe. A graduate of Lancaster University, the University of Durham and Ohio State University, Roger is currently Professor of Political Science at Cardiff University.

Roger is the author of several previous books, *Becoming Europeans? Attitudes, Behaviour, and Socialization in the European Parliament*, as well as *Representing Europe's Citizens? Electoral Institutions and the Failure of Parliamentary Representation*, and *Wales Says Yes: Devolution and the 2011 Welsh Referendum*. He has published more than fifty articles in major academic journals including the *British Journal of Political Science*, *Electoral Studies*, the *European Journal of Political Research*, *Legislative Studies Quarterly*, *Party Politics* and *Publius*, and has contributed chapters to thirty books.

Roger is director of the Welsh Election Study, associate editor of *Parliamentary Affairs*, a fellow of the Learned Society of Wales and of the Royal Statistical Society, and an academician of the Academy of Social Sciences. He is a regular commentator across national and international media, and also does political consultancy. In 2017, Roger was named Political Studies Communicator of the Year by the Political Studies Association of the United Kingdom, for 'the authoritative and tangible contribution he has made ... astutely conveying wider political issues and enhancing the public understanding of politics'.

You can find out more about his work on his website, www.rogerscully.com, or follow him on Twitter @Roger_Scully.

# INDEX

**352PP HARDBACK, £25**

The British Labour Party has been one of the key UK political institutions for the advancement of social change in the past century. Yet one critical aspect of its makeup has always been misunderstood, underplayed or misrepresented: its Britishness. Throughout the party's history, its Britishness has been an integral part of how it has governed, and done politics.

Moreover, over the past decade or so, a new mobilising form of national identity has emerged, one that has become increasingly problematic for Labour: that of Englishness. Indeed, there is some evidence that 'Englishness' is now displacing working-class identity as the major pull of loyalty and allegiance.

*The People's Flag and the Union Jack* argues that Labour's Britishness and its ambiguous relationship with issues of national identity matter more today than ever before, and will continue to matter for the foreseeable future, when the UK is in fundamental crisis and its place in the world, and very existence, open to doubt.

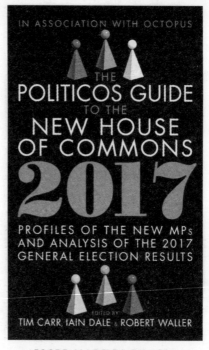

### 288PP PAPERBACK, £14.99

Even before soaring to the apparently impossible challenge of an outright majority at Holyrood in 2011, the Scottish National Party had long dominated the political narrative in Scotland. With the independence referendum in 2014 and their near clean sweep in the general election the following year, the full force of the SNP's power was felt throughout the UK. Now, with the party's rivals still trailing limply in their wake, this new account by two established SNP-watchers explains just how they have stormed to victory, changing the face of Scottish – and British – politics for ever.

Tracing the path from grassroots party of protest to professional, highly centralised electoral machine, Rob Johns and James Mitchell explore the differing leadership styles and often radical shifts in the party's image, from 'tartan Tories' to self-styled anti-austerity crusaders. Along the way, they analyse the internal battles between the leadership, members and activists; map the changing profile of the average SNP voter; and outline the new challenges that have come with increased electoral success.

Engaging, impartial and above all insightful, *Takeover* charts the rise and rise of Scotland's biggest party and asks: where now for the SNP in the wake of a historic third successive victory?

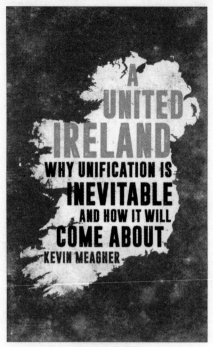

**256PP HARDBACK, £12.99**

For over two centuries, the 'Irish Question' has dogged British politics in one form or another – Northern Ireland's 'Troubles' being perhaps the bloodiest manifestation. And although the past twenty years have seen intensive efforts to secure a devolved local settlement via the Good Friday Agreement, its principle of consent – which holds that the country cannot leave the UK without a majority vote – has meant that the constitutional status of Northern Ireland remains moot.

Remote from the UK mainland in terms of its politics, economy and societal attitudes, Northern Ireland is placed, in effect, in an antechamber – subject to shifting demographic trends which are eroding the once-dominant Protestant Unionist majority, making a future referendum on the province's status a racing certainty. Indeed, in the light of Brexit and a highly probable second independence referendum in Scotland, the reunification of Ireland is not a question of 'if', but 'when' – and 'how'.

In *A United Ireland*, Kevin Meagher argues that a reasoned, pragmatic discussion about Britain's relationship with its nearest neighbour is now long overdue, and questions that have remained unasked (and perhaps unthought) must now be answered.